WHO

WAS BJORN FAULKNER?

To the world, he was a startlingly successful international tycoon, head of a vast financial empire.

To his beautiful secretary-mistress, he was a god-like hero to be served with her mind, soul, and body.

To his aristocratic young wife, he was an elemental force of nature to be tamed.

To his millionaire father-in-law, he was a giant whose single error could be used to destroy him.

What kind of man was Bjorn Faulkner? Only you, the reader, can decide.

TITLES BY AYN RAND
FROM NEW AMERICAN LIBRARY

Anthem

Atlas Shrugged

Capitalism: The Unknown Ideal

For The New Intellectual

The Fountainhead

Introduction to Objectivist Epistemology

The New Left: The Anti-Industrial Revolution

Night of January 16th

Philosophy: Who Needs It

The Romantic Manifesto

The Virtue of Selfishness

We The Living

Night of January 16th

A *Play by* AYN RAND

THE FINAL REVISED VERSION

A PLUME BOOK

PLUME
Published by the Penguin Group
Penguin Books USA Inc., 375 Hudson Street, New York, New York
10014, U.S.A.
Penguin Books Ltd, 27 Wrights Lane, London W8 5TZ, England
Penguin Books Australia Ltd, Ringwood, Victoria, Australia
Penguin Books Canada Ltd, 2801 John Street, Markham, Ontario,
Canada L3R 1B4
Penguin Books (N.Z.) Ltd, 182-190 Wairau Road, Auckland 10, New
Zealand

Penguin Books Ltd, Registered Offices: Harmondsworth, Middlesex,
England

Published by Plume, an imprint of New American Library, a division of
Penguin Books USA Inc.

 REGISTERED TRADEMARK—MARCA REGISTRADA

Library of Congress Cataloging-in-Publication Data

Rand, Ayn.
  Night of January 16th.

  I. Title.
PS3535.A547N5   1987   812'.54   87-5805
ISBN 0-452-26486-3

FIRST SIGNET PRINTING, JANUARY, 1971
FIRST PLUME PRINTING, FEBRUARY, 1987

9   10   11   12

PRINTED IN THE UNITED STATES OF AMERICA

Night of
January 16th

INTRODUCTION

IF I WERE TO CLASSIFY *Night of January 16th* in conventional literary terms, I would say that it represents, not Romantic Realism, but Romantic Symbolism. For those acquainted with Objectivist aesthetics, I can name a more precise classification: *Night of January 16th* is not a philosophical, but a sense-of-life play.

A sense of life is a preconceptual equivalent of metaphysics, an emotional, subconsciously integrated appraisal of *man's relationship to existence.* I emphasize this last because it is a man's attitude toward life that constitutes the core and motor of his subconscious philosophy. Every work of fiction (and wider: every work of art) is the product and expression of its author's sense of life. But it may express that sense of life translated into conceptual, i.e., philosophical, terms, or it may express only an abstract emotional sum. *Night of January 16th* is a pure, untranslated abstraction.

This means that its events are not to be taken *literally;* they dramatize certain fundamental psychological characteristics, deliberately isolated and emphasized in order to convey a single abstraction: the characters' attitude toward life. The

1

events serve to feature the *motives* of the characters' actions, regardless of the particular forms of
action—i.e., the motives, not their specific con-
cretization. The events feature the confrontation
of two extremes, two opposite ways of facing existence: passionate self-assertiveness, self-confidence, ambition, audacity, independence—versus
conventionality, servility, envy, hatred, power-lust.

I do not think, nor did I think it when I wrote this
play, that a swindler is a heroic character or that a
respectable banker is a villain. But for the purpose
of dramatizing the conflict of independence versus
conformity, a criminal—a social outcast—can be
an eloquent symbol. This, incidentally, is the reason of the profound appeal of the "noble crook" in
fiction. He is the symbol of the rebel as such,
regardless of the kind of society he rebels against,
the symbol—for most people—of their vague, un-
defined, unrealized groping toward a concept, or a
shadowy image, of man's self-esteem.

That a career of crime is not, in fact, the way
to implement one's self-esteem, is irrelevant in
sense-of-life terms. A sense of life is concerned
primarily with consciousness, not with existence
—or rather: with the way a man's consciousness
faces existence. It is concerned with a basic frame
of mind, not with rules of conduct.

If this play's sense of life were to be verbalized,
it would say, in effect: "Your life, your achieve-
ment, your happiness, *your person* are of paramount importance. Live up to your highest vision of
yourself no matter what the circumstances you
might encounter. An exalted view of self-esteem is
a man's most admirable quality." How one is to
live up to this vision—how this frame of mind
is to be implemented in action and in reality—is

a question that a sense of life cannot answer: *that* is the task of philosophy.*

Night of January 16th is not a philosophical treatise on morality: that basic frame of mind (and its opposite) is all that I wanted to convey.

This play was written in 1933. It started in my mind with the idea of writing a courtroom drama, a murder trial, in which the jury would be drawn from the audience and would vote on the verdict. Obviously, the factual evidence of the defendant's guilt or innocence had to be evenly balanced in order to make either verdict possible. But a jury's disagreement about inconclusive facts could not be of any possible interest or significance. The issue at stake, therefore, had to be psychological.

The springboard for the story was the collapse of Ivar Kreuger—or, more precisely, the public reaction to that collapse.

On March 12, 1932, Ivar Kreuger, the Swedish "Match King," committed suicide. His death was followed by the crash of the vast financial empire he had created, and by the revelation that that empire was a gigantic fraud. He had been a mysterious figure, a "lone wolf," celebrated as a man of genius, of unswerving determination and spectacular audacity. His fall was like an explosion that threw up a storm of dust and muck—a storm of peculiarly virulent denunciations.

It was not his shady methods, his ruthlessness, his dishonesty that were being denounced, but his *ambition*. His ability, his self-confidence, the glamorous aura of his life and name were featured,

---

*For a fuller discussion of the nature and functions of a sense of life, I refer you to my articles, "Philosophy and Sense of Life" and "Art and Sense of Life," in my book *The Romantic Manifesto*.

exaggerated, overstressed, to serve as fodder for the hordes of envious mediocrities rejoicing at his downfall. It was a spree of gloating malice. Its leitmotif was not: "How did he fall?" but: "How did he dare to rise?" Had there been a world press at the time of Icarus and Phaëthon, *this* was the kind of obituary they would have received.

In fact, Ivar Kreuger was a man of unusual ability who had, at first, made a fortune by legitimate means; it was his venture into politics—mixed-economy politics—that destroyed him. Seeking a world monopoly for his match industry, he began to give large loans to various European governments in exchange for a monopoly status in their countries—loans which were not repaid, which he could not collect and which led him to a fantastic juggling of his assets and bookkeeping in order to conceal his losses. In the final analysis, it was not Kreuger who profiteered on the ruin of the investors he had swindled; the profiteers were sundry European governments. (But when governments pursue such policies, it is not called a swindle: it is called "deficit financing.")

At the time of Kreuger's death, it was not the political aspects of his story that interested me, but the nature of those public denunciations. It was not a crook that they were denouncing, but greatness as such; it was greatness as such that I wanted to defend.

This, then, was my assignment in *Night of January 16th:* to dramatize the sense of life that was vaguely symbolized by Ivar Kreuger, and set it against the sense of life blatantly revealed by his attackers.

Bjorn Faulkner, the hero who never appears in the play, is not Ivar Kreuger; he is what Ivar

Kreuger might have been or, perhaps, ought to have been. The two sides in the play are represented, on the one hand, by Bjorn Faulkner and Karen Andre, his secretary-mistress who is on trial for his murder—and, on the other, by John Graham Whitfield and his daughter. The factual evidence for and against the accused is (approximately) balanced. The issue rests on the credibility of the witnesses. The jury has to choose which side to believe, and this depends on every juror's own sense of life.

Or, at least, so I hoped. I was aware, even then, that most people would not see the issue in such terms, that most people are not that consistent, neither in their conscious convictions, nor in their choice of values, nor even in their sense of life. I was aware that they would probably miss the basic antithesis and would judge on the spur or color or drama of the moment, attaching no further significance to their verdict.

I knew also that a sense-of-life issue was not the best way to implement the idea of a trial by an audience-jury, and that some explicit controversial issue would be better, such as birth control or mercy-killing or "trial marriages." But here I truly had no choice. For the life of me, I could not have invented a story dealing with some narrow issue. My own sense of life demanded a theme involving great figures and crucial fundamentals; I could not arouse myself to any interest in anything less—then or now.

The motive of my writing has always been the presentation of an ideal man. I did not regard Bjorn Faulkner as an ideal. But I was not ready to attempt the portrait of an ideal man; his first appearance in my writing is Howard Roark in *The*

Fountainhead, followed by the heroes of *Atlas Shrugged*. What I *was* ready to write about was a woman's feeling for her ideal man, and this I did in the person of Karen Andre.

Those interested in tracing my personal development will observe the sense-of-life consistency of this play with my subsequent novels. But my novels deal with more than a sense of life: they involve a conscious philosophy, i.e., a conceptually defined view of man and of existence. And, to illustrate the translation of a sense of life into conceptual terms: if Bjorn Faulkner were to make the same mistakes in terms applicable to actual life, he would become Gail Wynand, the most tragic character in *The Fountainhead;* or, if Bjorn Faulkner were to be an ideal businessman, he would become Francisco d'Anconia of *Atlas Shrugged.*

I am still asked, once in a while—and it always astonishes me—whether I intended Karen Andre to be found guilty or not guilty. I did not think that there could be any doubt about *my* verdict: of course, *she is not guilty.* (But this need not deter any prospective viewer or reader from pronouncing his own judgment: in this matter, to each his own sense of life.)

The original title of this play was *Penthouse Legend.*

This is still its best title; it gives some indication of the play's nonrealistic, symbolic nature. But it was changed twice, first to *Woman on Trial*, then to *Night of January 16th.* In both cases, the producers assured me that my original title would be a serious handicap to the play; one of them claimed that the public was antagonized by the word "Legend" and he cited the failure of some movies which had used that word in their titles. I thought that this was nonsense, but I did not want the producers to work under the pressure of doubt or fear in regard to an issue about which they felt very strongly, but which I considered unimportant.

Today, I regret it. *Night of January 16th* is an empty, meaningless title. It was, however, the least offensive one of those suggested to me at the time. I could not change it later: the play had become too famous.

In a way, that title is appropriate to the practical history of the play: for me, it was empty, meaningless—and very painful.

The play's history began with a series of rejections by New York's theatrical producers. I was living in Hollywood at the time, but I had an agent who kept sending the play to one producer after another. What I regarded as the most original feature of the play was the idea of drawing the jury from the audience. It was precisely because of this idea that the producers rejected the play: the jury gimmick would not work, they said, the public would not go for it, it would "destroy the theatrical illusion."

Then, simultaneously, I received two offers for the play: one from A. H. Woods, a well-known New York producer, the other from E. E. Clive, a British actor who ran a modest stock company at the Hollywood Playhouse. But Woods wanted the right to make changes in my play at his sole discretion. So I rejected his offer and signed a contract with Clive.

The play was produced at the Hollywood Playhouse in the fall of 1934, under the title *Woman on Trial*. The role of Karen Andre was played by

Barbara Bedford, a star of the silent movies. E. E.
Clive directed it and played a small part; he was a
brilliant character actor, who loved my play and
seemed to understand it, at least to the extent of
knowing that there was something unusual about
it. To this day, I deeply appreciate his attitude.
But, as a producer, he was badly handicapped by
lack of funds. The production was competent, but
somewhat unexciting: unstylized and too natural-
istic. The play received good reviews and had a
modestly successful run.

At its conclusion, A. H. Woods renewed his
offer for a Broadway production. The contract
clause regarding script changes was reworded, but
in a highly ambiguous manner; my agent assured
me that the new clause meant that all changes
were to be made by mutual consent. I did not
think so; I was fairly certain that it still gave
Woods the control he wanted, but I decided to
take the chance, relying on nothing but my power
of persuasion.

The rest of the play's history was hell.

The entire period before and after the play's
opening was a sickening struggle between Woods
and me. I managed to prevent the worst of the
changes he wanted to introduce, and I managed
to preserve the best of the passages he wanted to
eliminate, but that was all I could do. So the play
became an incongruous mongrel slapdashed out of
contradictory elements.

Woods was famous as a producer of melodra-
mas, some of which had been good, some dreadful.
Melodrama was the only element of my play that
he understood, but he thought that there wasn't
enough of it. So, "to liven it up," he introduced,
in small touches, a junk heap of worn, irrelevant

melodramatic devices that clashed with the style, did not advance the action and served only to confuse the audience—such as a gun, a heat test to determine its erased serial number, a flashy gun moll, etc. (The gun moll was introduced, in the last act, to throw doubt on the testimony of Guts Regan, which, of course, she did not accomplish. I did not write that bit; it was written by the play's director.) Woods actually believed that only guns, fingerprints and police matters could hold an audience's attention, but "speeches" could not. To his credit as a showman, I can say only that he thought the jury gimmick was a great idea, which is what made him buy the play.

This was my first (but not last) encounter with the literary manifestation of the mind-body dichotomy that dominates today's culture: the split between the "serious" and the "entertaining"—the belief that if a literary work is "serious," it must bore people to death; and if it is "entertaining," it must not communicate anything of importance. (Which means that "the good" has to be painful, and that pleasure has to be mindlessly low-grade.) A. H. Woods was a faithful adherent of that school of thought, so that it was useless to mention the word "thought" to him, or "idea" or "philosophy" or "sense of life" in connection with any theatrical matter. It would be inexact to say that he was antagonistic to such concepts: he was completely tone-deaf to them. I was naive enough to be shocked by it. Since then, I have observed the same tone-deafness in regard to this dichotomy (though, usually, on its other side) in men who had less excuse for it than A. H. Woods: in college professors. At the time, I fought against that dogma to the limit of my brain and endurance. I am still fighting that battle today, with the same intensity, but without the painful, incredulous astonishment of youth.

In regard to casting, Woods' judgment was better than his literary views. He gave the part of Karen Andre to a talented unknown, a young actress he had discovered—Doris Nolan. She was very attractive in the right way, she was an unusually good type for the part and gave an excellent performance. The male lead, the part of Guts Regan, was played by Walter Pidgeon. This was my one contribution to the casting. At that time, which was the period of transition from the silent movies to the talkies, Pidgeon was regarded as through in Hollywood and was playing in a summer stock theater in the East. He had been one of my favorites in the silent movies (where he had played strong, glamorous, aristocratic villains) and I had seen him on the stage in Hollywood, so I suggested that Woods go to see him in summer stock. Woods' first reaction was: "Aw, he's through," but he went. To give him credit, Woods was so impressed with Pidgeon's performance that he signed him for *Night of January 16th* at once (and told me: "Aw, that guy's great"). Shortly after our opening, Pidgeon signed a long-term movie contract with M-G-M, which was his new start in pictures, the beginning of his rise to stardom. He told me later that he owed that contract to his performance as Guts Regan. (I regret that M-G-M confined him to the homey, "*Mister* Miniver" type of role; he deserved better than that.)

This was one of the few pleasant incidents connected with *Night of January 16th*. By the time the play opened on Broadway (in September of 1935), it was dead, as far as I was concerned. I could feel nothing for it or about it except revulsion and indignation. It was not merely a mangled body, but worse: it was a mangled body with some of its torn limbs still showing a former beauty and underscoring the bloody mess. On opening night, I sat in the back row, yawning—not out of tension, but out of genuine boredom, since it was an event that had no value-meaning for me any longer.

The play received mixed reviews; it did not become a hit, but what was regarded as a "success." It ran for six months. What made it successful and talked about was, of course, the jury gimmick. On opening night, Woods had arranged in advance for a jury of celebrities (of whom the only one I remember was Jack Dempsey, the former heavyweight champion). For the first couple of weeks thereafter, he kept a jury of stooges on hand backstage, just in case the members of the audience did not volunteer. But he soon found the precaution unnecessary: his office was besieged by requests from celebrities and others who wanted to sit on that jury; there were more volunteers than he could accommodate.

One interesting incident of the play's run was a benefit performance given for the blind. (I did not attend it: I could not bear to see the play again, but I was told about it.) All the members of the jury and most of the audience were blind; the foreman of the jury was Helen Keller. Graham McNamee, a famous newscaster, acted as a narrator to describe visual information, when needed. The verdict that night was "Guilty."

As to the general record of verdicts during the play's run in New York, they were 3 to 2 in favor

of acquittal—according to the stage manager, who
kept a tally.

That winter, Woods launched two road companies (starting out of Chicago and Los Angeles)
and a third company in London; all of them did
very well.

The Chicago production remains in my mind for
the unexpected reason that a drama critic, Ashton Stevens, gave me the only review that pleased
me in my entire career. I have received reviews
that might be called better and some that I deeply
appreciated, but none of them said the things I
would have wanted to be said. I learned to expect
nothing from reviewers because of the so-called fa-
vorable reviews, not because of the illiterate
smears. What I liked about Ashton Stevens' piece
was that he understood the *technique* of drama,
knew what it takes and praised me for the best
aspects of the play's structure; he praised me for
an attribute which only a viewer in full focus can
appreciate: ingenuity. He treated the play as a
melodrama, since that is all it had become; I am
inclined to believe that his sense of life was probably
the opposite of mine, since he wrote: "It is not as
close and upclimbing a piece as [*The Trial of*] *Mary
Dugan*. Nor as heart-tearing. None of the characters
is lovable."

But here is what I love *him* for: "But it is the
fastest courtroom melo I ever saw. It shoots its
stuff from a dozen angles, and every shot is a
surprise.

"The biggest and best surprise is when the
prisoner—the tense, Roman-medal-faced Karen
Andre—crashes and crumbles as Gunman ('Guts')
Regan rushes up the aisle and into court and in-
forms her that the man she is accused of murder-

ing IS dead. That, ladies and gentlemen of the audience, is a S E C O N D-A C T C U R T A I N. [Typography his.] . . .

"You see, the play flattered the cunning of the audience. It permitted us to anticipate with some success. But it never left us right for more than a jiffy. . . . There is a kind of genius in the play." (If there was, in the version he saw, I marvel at his ability to see it.)

The play was unusually successful in summer stock: in its first summer (1936), it was presented by eighteen theaters, and was a leading favorite for many summers thereafter. One bright spot of the summer of 1936 was a week at a theater in Stony Creek, Connecticut, where the part of Guts Regan was played by my husband, Frank O'Connor.

In subsequent years, the play was presented, in various translations, in most European countries. In World War II, it was presented by the U.S.O. for the American troops occupying Berlin. It is still being given occasionally in various parts of the world, with or without my knowledge; at least, I receive unexpected royalties from it, once in a while. And, once in a while, it is still played here, in summer stock. It has been presented on the radio and twice (by two different companies) on television.

The amateur market of this play belongs on the horror side of its history. The amateur rights were sold to a publishing house that issued an adapted, "cleaned up" version. The amateur market, they claimed at the time, consisted of church, school and college groups that worked under a strict kind of censorship (I do not know who imposed it): these groups were not allowed to mention a love affair or a mistress, or to smoke onstage, or to swear, etc. For instance, they were not allowed to use the word "Guts," so that my character's name was changed to "Larry" Regan. That version of my play was adapted by the publishing house; it was not to be sold in bookstores or to the public, but was to be sold *only* to amateur groups for amateur performances. Once in a while, I hear— with somewhat helpless indignation—that some fan of mine has somehow obtained a copy of that version. So I want to state formally, for the record and as a public notice, that the amateur version of *Night of January 16th* is not written by me and is not part of my works.

The movie version of this play is another horror story. I had nothing to do with its screen adaptation. There is nothing of mine in that movie, except the names of some of the characters and the title (which was not mine). The *only* line of dialogue from my play which appears in the movie is: "The court will now adjourn till ten o'clock tomorrow morning." The cheap, trashy vulgarity of that movie is such that no lengthier discussion is possible to me.

Through all those years, while the play was becoming famous, I felt a painfully growing embarrassment: I did not want to be associated with it or to be known as its author. I thought, at the time, that I had merely been unlucky in my producer and in the kind of people I had to deal with. Today, I know better: I know that it could not have been different, granting the nature of my work and of today's cultural trends. But don't let anyone ever approach me about making changes in my work: I learned my lesson the hard way.

For twenty-five years, I never looked at a script

of this play, and winced whenever it was mentioned. Then, in 1960, Nathaniel Branden asked me to let him give a reading of the play at Nathaniel Branden Institute, in response to requests from students. I could not let him read the A. H. Woods version, so I had to prepare a definitive version of the play. I compared the original script of *Penthouse Legend*, the script of *Woman on Trial* (which was the same, but with some cuts made by me) and the script of *Night of January 16th*. I was somewhat astonished by the result: in this final, definitive version, I had to cut out *everything* that had been contributed by the Woods production (except one line change and the title). I cut out, of course, the gun moll, the gun and all the cruder elements of that sort; but I did not expect to find that even small lines and minor touches were jarringly wrong and had to be discarded.

I felt an odd kind of sadness: my mind went back to a certain argument I had with Woods during the rehearsals. We were sitting in the front row of an empty theater and he was saying indignantly: "How can you be so stubborn? How can you argue with me? This is your first play and I've been in the theater for forty years!" I explained to him that it was not a matter of personalities, age or experience, not a matter of *who* said it, but of *what* was said, and that I would give in to his office boy, if the boy happened to be *right*. Woods did not answer; I knew even then that he did not hear me.

The final, definitive version of *Night of January 16th* is closest, in content, to the script of *Woman on Trial*. I made no changes in story or substance; the additional changes I made were mainly grammatical. That final version is the one now published here, in this book.

I am glad to see it published. Up to now, I had felt as if it were an illegitimate child roaming the world. Now, with this publication, it becomes legitimately mine.

And, although it has played all over the world, I feel as if it were a play that has never been produced.

AYN RAND

New York, June 1968

A note from Ayn Rand's Executor:

In 1973, for a production of *Night of January 16th* under the title of *Penthouse Legend,* Ayn Rand made several dozen relatively small editorial changes in the text of the play, mostly with a view to updating the language. Judging from correspondence of hers that has recently been discovered, Miss Rand regarded these changes as definitive. They are, therefore, being incorporated in all future printings, beginning with this one.

Leonard Peikoff
May 1985

NOTE TO PRODUCER

THIS PLAY is a murder trial without a pre-arranged verdict. The jurors are to be selected from the audience. They are to witness the play as real jurors and bring in a verdict at the end of the last act. Two short endings are written for the play—to be used according to the verdict.

The play is built in such a way that the evidence of the defendant's guilt or innocence is evenly balanced and the decision will have to be based upon the jurors' own values and characters. The two parties opposed in the trial are as radically antagonistic as will be members of any audience, where some will sympathize with the wife, others with the mistress. Either decision will bring the protest of the opposite side; the case is bound to arouse arguments and discussions, for its underlying conflict is the basic conflict of two different types of humanity. It is really the audience who is thus put on trial. In the words of the defense attorney: "Who is on trial in this case? Karen Andre? No! It's you, ladies and gentlemen of the jury, who are here on trial. It is your own souls that will be brought to light when your decision is rendered."

The jurors' seats are to be on the stage, as in a real courtroom. Thus we give the public all the excitement of a murder trial. We heighten the public's interest by leaving the decision in its own hands and add to the suspense by the fact that no audience, at any performance of the play, can be sure of its outcome.

Characters

JUDGE HEATH

DISTRICT ATTORNEY FLINT

DEFENSE ATTORNEY STEVENS

KAREN ANDRE

DR. KIRKLAND

JOHN HUTCHINS

HOMER VAN FLEET

ELMER SWEENEY

MAGDA SVENSON

NANCY LEE FAULKNER

JOHN GRAHAM WHITFIELD

JAMES CHANDLER

SIEGURD JUNGQUIST

"GUTS" REGAN

COURT ATTENDANTS

TIME: *Present*

PLACE: *New York Courtroom*

Act One

SCENE: *The stage represents a New York courtroom. It faces the audience, so that the public is in the position of spectators in a real courtroom. In the center of the back is the Judge's desk on a high platform; behind it is the door to the Judge's chambers; by the side of the desk, at left, is the witness stand, facing the audience; behind it is the door to the jury room. In front of the Judge's desk is the desk of the Court Reporter; at right—the desk of the Court Clerk. Behind it is the door through which witnesses enter the courtroom. Farther downstage, at right, is a table for the defendant and attorneys; at left —another table for the prosecution. At the wall, left, are the twelve seats for the jurors. Farther downstage is a door through which spectators enter the courtroom. At the opposite wall, at right, are a few chairs for spectators. Steps lead down from the stage in the right and left aisles. When the curtain rises the court session is ready to open, but the JUDGE has not yet made his appearance. The prosecution and defense are ready at their respective tables.*

DISTRICT ATTORNEY FLINT *is a heavy, middle-aged man with the kindly appearance of a re-*

21

spectable father of a family and the shrewd,
piercing manner of a pawnbroker. DEFENSE AT-
TORNEY STEVENS *is tall, gray-haired, displaying*
the grooming and sophisticated grace of a man
of the world. He is watching his client, who does
not pay any attention to him and, sitting at the
defense table, calmly, almost insolently studies
the audience. The client, the defendant KAREN
ANDRE, *is twenty-eight. One's first impression of*
her is that to handle her would require the serv-
ices of an animal trainer, not an attorney. Yet
there is nothing emotional or rebellious in her
countenance; it is one of profound, inexorable
calm; but one feels the tense vitality, the primi-
tive fire, the untamed strength in the defiant im-
mobility of her slender body, the proud line of her
head held high, the sweep of her tousled hair. Her
clothes are conspicuous by their severe, tailored
simplicity; a very costly simplicity, one can no-
tice, but not the elegance of a woman who gives
much thought to her clothes; rather that of one
who knows she can make any rag attractive and
does it unconsciously.

When the curtain rises the lights in the audience
do not go out.

BAILIFF: Court attention!

[EVERYONE *rises as* JUDGE HEATH *enters.* BAILIFF
raps]

Superior Court Number Eleven of the State of
New York. The Honorable Judge William Heath
presiding.

[*The* JUDGE *takes his seat.* BAILIFF *raps and*
EVERYONE *sits down*]

JUDGE HEATH: The people of the State of New York versus Karen Andre.

FLINT: Ready, your Honor.

STEVENS: Ready, your Honor.

JUDGE HEATH: Mr. Clerk, draw a jury.

[*The* CLERK *steps to the proscenium with a list in his hand, and addresses the audience*]

CLERK: Ladies and gentlemen, you are to be the jurors in this case. Twelve of you will be drawn to perform this duty. You will kindly step up here, take your seats, and receive your instructions from Judge Heath.
[*He reads twelve names. The* JURORS *take their places. If some are unwilling and do not appear, the* CLERK *calls a few more names. When the jurors are seated, the lights in the audience go out.* JUDGE HEATH *addresses the jury*]

JUDGE HEATH: Ladies and gentlemen, you are the jurors who will try this case. At its close, you will retire to the jury room and vote upon your verdict. At the end of each day's session, you will remain seated until the Bailiff escorts you to the jury room. I instruct you to listen to the testimony carefully and pronounce your judgment to the best of your ability and integrity. You are to determine whether the defendant is Guilty or Not Guilty and her fate rests in your hands . . . The District Attorney may now proceed.

[DISTRICT ATTORNEY FLINT *rises and addresses the jury*]

FLINT: Your Honor! Ladies and gentlemen of the jury! On the sixteenth of January, near midnight, when the lights of Broadway blazed an electric dawn over the festive crowds below, the body of a man came hurtling through space and crashed—a disfigured mess—at the foot of the Faulkner Building. That body had been Sweden's great financier—Bjorn Faulkner. He fell fifty stories from his luxurious penthouse. *A suicide,* we were told. A great man unwilling to bend before his imminent ruin. A man who found a fall from the roof of a skyscraper shorter and easier than a descent from his tottering throne of the world's financial dictator. Only a few months ago, behind every big transaction of gold in the world, stood that well-known figure: young, tall, with an arrogant smile, with kingdoms and nations in the palm of one hand—and a whip in the other. If gold is the world's life blood, then Bjorn Faulkner, holding all its dark, hidden arteries, regulating its ebb and flow, its every pulsation, was the heart of the world. Well, ladies and gentlemen, the world has just had a heart attack. And like all heart attacks, it was rather sudden. No one suspected the gigantic swindle that lay at the foundation of the Faulkner enterprises. A few days after his death, the earth shook from the crash of his business; thousands of investors were stricken with the paralysis which follows an attack, when that monstrous heart stopped beating. Bjorn Faulkner had had a hard struggle facing the world. But he had a much harder struggle to face in his heart, a struggle which this trial will have to uncover. Two women ruled his life—and death. Here is one of them, ladies and gentlemen.

[*Points at* KAREN]

Karen Andre, Faulkner's efficient secretary and notorious mistress. But six months ago Faulkner

came to America to get a loan and save his fortune. Fate sent him a means to save his own heart
—in the person of the lovely girl who is now his
widow, Nancy Lee Faulkner, only daughter of
John Graham Whitfield, our great philanthropist.
Faulkner thought he had found salvation and a
new life in the virtuous innocence of his young
bride. And the best proof of it is that two weeks
after his wedding he dismissed his secretary—
Karen Andre. He was through with her. But,
ladies and gentlemen, one is not easily through
with a woman like Karen Andre. We can only
guess at what hatred and revenge smouldered in
her heart; but they leaped into flame on the *night
of January sixteenth*. Bjorn Faulkner *did not* kill
himself. He was murdered. Murdered by the very
delicate and capable hands which you see here
before you.

[*He points at* KAREN]

The hands that helped to raise Bjorn Faulkner
high over the world; the hands that threw him
down, from as great a height, to crash into a pavement cold as this woman's heart. That, ladies and
gentlemen, is what we are going to prove.

[FLINT *pauses; then calls*]

Our first witness will be Doctor Kirkland.

CLERK: Dr. Kirkland!

[DR. KIRKLAND, *elderly, kindly, and indifferent,
makes his way toward the witness stand*]

CLERK: You solemnly swear to tell the truth, the
whole truth and nothing but the truth so help
you God?

KIRKLAND: I do.

FLINT: Kindly state your name.

KIRKLAND: Thomas Kirkland.

FLINT: What is your occupation?

KIRKLAND: Medical examiner of this county.

FLINT: In the course of your duty, what were you called upon to do on the night of January sixteenth?

KIRKLAND: I was called to examine the body of Bjorn Faulkner.

FLINT: What did you find?

KIRKLAND: A body mangled to an extreme degree.

FLINT: What did you establish as the cause of death?

KIRKLAND: A fall from a great height.

FLINT: How long had Faulkner been dead when you examined his body?

KIRKLAND: I reached it about half an hour after the fall.

FLINT: Judging by the condition of the body, could you say exactly how long it had been dead?

KIRKLAND: No, I could not. Owing to the cold weather, the blood had coagulated immediately, which makes a difference of several hours impossible to detect.

FLINT: Therefore, it is possible that Faulkner had been dead longer than half an hour?

KIRKLAND: It is possible.

FLINT: Could his death have been caused by anything other than this fall?

KIRKLAND: I found no evidence of it.

FLINT: For instance, had his skull been broken before the fall, would you be able to tell it by examining the body?

KIRKLAND: No. Owing to the condition of the body, it would be impossible to determine.

FLINT: That's all, Doctor.

STEVENS: Did you find any trace of any such earlier wound in your examination of the body, Doctor Kirkland?

KIRKLAND: No, I did not.

STEVENS: Did you find any indication that death might have been caused by anything other than the fall?

KIRKLAND: No, I did not.

STEVENS: That's all.

[DR. KIRKLAND *leaves the stand and exits*]

FLINT: John Hutchins!

CLERK: John Hutchins!

[HUTCHINS *is a timid, elderly man, neat, but almost shabby; he walks to the stand shyly, cringing, nervously fingering his hat in both hands*]

CLERK: You solemnly swear to tell the truth, the whole truth and nothing but the truth so help you God?

HUTCHINS: Yes, sir, I do.

FLINT: What is your name?

HUTCHINS: [*Timidly*] John Joseph Hutchins.

FLINT: And your occupation?

HUTCHINS: I'm the night watchman in the Faulkner Building, sir.

FLINT: Did Mr. Faulkner have business offices in that building?

HUTCHINS: Yes, sir.

FLINT: Do you know who owned the penthouse on the roof of the building?

HUTCHINS: Certainly, sir. Mr. Faulkner did.

FLINT: And who lived there?

HUTCHINS: Mr. Faulkner and Miss Andre, sir. That is, before Mr. Faulkner's marriage.

FLINT: And after the marriage?

HUTCHINS: After the marriage, Miss Andre lived there—alone.

FLINT: Have you ever seen Mr. Faulkner calling on Miss Andre after his marriage?

HUTCHINS: Only once, sir.

FLINT: And that was?

HUTCHINS: On the night of January sixteenth.

FLINT: Tell us about it, Mr. Hutchins.

HUTCHINS: Well, sir, it was about ten thirty and—

FLINT: How did you know the time?

HUTCHINS: I come on duty at ten, sir, and it was

no more than a half hour after. The entrance door bell rang. I went down to the lobby and opened the door. It was Miss Andre, and Mr. Faulkner was with her. I was surprised, because Miss Andre has her own key and, usually, she opens the door herself.

FLINT: Was she alone with Mr. Faulkner?

HUTCHINS: No, sir. There were two other gentlemen with them.

FLINT: Who were they?

HUTCHINS: I don't know, sir.

FLINT: Had you ever seen them before?

HUTCHINS: No, sir, never.

FLINT: What did they look like?

HUTCHINS: They were tall and sort of slender, both of them. One had sharp cheekbones, as I remember. The other one—I couldn't see his face at all, sir, on account of his hat being all crooked over his eyes. He must have had a bit too much, sir, meaning no disrespect.

FLINT: Just what do you mean?

HUTCHINS: Well, he was a bit tight, sir, if I'm permitted to say so. He wasn't very steady on his feet, so that Mr. Faulkner and the other gentleman had to help him. They almost dragged him into the elevator.

FLINT: Did Mr. Faulkner look worried?

HUTCHINS: No, sir. On the contrary, he seemed very happy.

FLINT: Did he look like a man contemplating suicide?

STEVENS: We object, your Honor!

JUDGE HEATH: Objection sustained.

FLINT: Did the others in the party seem happy, too?

HUTCHINS: Yes, sir. Miss Andre was smiling. And Mr. Faulkner laughed when they went up in the elevator.

FLINT: Did you see any of them leave, that night?

HUTCHINS: Yes, sir. The first one left about fifteen minutes later.

FLINT: Who was that?

HUTCHINS: The drunken one, sir. He came down in the elevator, all by himself. He didn't seem quite so drunk no more. He could walk, but he staggered a little.

FLINT: Did you see where he went?

HUTCHINS: Well, I wanted to help him to the door, seeing the condition he was in, but he noticed me coming and he hurried out. He got into a car parked right at the entrance and did he step on it! But I'm sure he didn't go far. The cops must've got him.

FLINT: What makes you think that?

HUTCHINS: Well, I noticed a car that started right after him.

[KAREN *comes to life, suddenly, out of her frozen calm. She jumps up and throws her question at Hutchins*]

KAREN: What car?

JUDGE HEATH: The defendant will please keep quiet.

[STEVENS *whispers to* KAREN, *making her sit down*]

FLINT: If Miss Andre will let me do the questioning, I may satisfy her curiosity. I was just going to ask what car, Mr. Hutchins?

HUTCHINS: It was a big black sedan, sir. It was parked two cars away from him.

FLINT: Who was in it?

HUTCHINS: I saw only one man.

FLINT: What makes you think he was after the first car?

HUTCHINS: Well, I couldn't be sure he was, sir. It just looked funny they started together like that.

FLINT: Did you see that other guest of Miss Andre's leaving, too?

HUTCHINS: Yes, sir. It wasn't more than ten minutes later when he came out of the elevator.

FLINT: What did he do?

HUTCHINS: Nothing unusual, sir. He seemed to be in a hurry. He went right out.

FLINT: And then what happened?

HUTCHINS: I started on my round of the building; and then, it must have been an hour later, I heard screams outside, in the street. I rushed down and as I came into the lobby, I saw Miss

Andre running out of the elevator, her gown all torn, sobbing wild-like. I ran after her. We pushed through the crowd outside and *there* was Mr. Faulkner all over the pavement.

FLINT: What did Miss Andre do?

HUTCHINS: She screamed and fell on her knees. It was horrible, sir. I've never seen a body smashed like that.

FLINT: That is all, Mr. Hutchins.

STEVENS: You said that you had never seen Mr. Faulkner calling on Miss Andre after his marriage, with the exception of that night. Now, tell me, do you always see every visitor who comes into the building at night?

HUTCHINS: No, sir. I'm not in the lobby all of the time, I have my rounds to make. If the guest has a key, he can come in and I wouldn't see him at all.

STEVENS: In other words, Miss Andre might have had any number of visitors, Mr. Faulkner included, whom you never saw come in?

HUTCHINS: Yes, sir, quite right.

STEVENS: That is all.

[HUTCHINS *leaves the stand and exits*]

FLINT: Homer Van Fleet!

CLERK: Homer Van Fleet!

[HOMER VAN FLEET *makes his appearance. He is tall, not very young, and can be best described by the word "correct." His clothes are correct—smart, but not flashy; his manner is*

*correct—cool, exact, strictly businesslike. He is
diffident and dignified at the same time*]

CLERK: You solemnly swear to tell the truth, the
whole truth and nothing but the truth so help
you God?

VAN FLEET: I do.

FLINT: Your name?

VAN FLEET: Homer Herbert Van Fleet.

FLINT: Occupation?

VAN FLEET: Private investigator.

FLINT: What was your last assignment?

VAN FLEET: Shadowing Mr. Bjorn Faulkner.

FLINT: By whom were you hired to do it?

VAN FLEET: By Mrs. Bjorn Faulkner.

[*A slight reaction in the courtroom*]

FLINT: Were you shadowing Mr. Faulkner on the
night of January sixteenth?

VAN FLEET: I was.

FLINT: Kindly tell us about it.

VAN FLEET: I'll start with six thirteen P.M.

FLINT: How do you know the time, Mr. Van
Fleet?

VAN FLEET: Part of my duties. Had to record it
and report to Mrs. Faulkner.

FLINT: I see.

VAN FLEET: [*He speaks briskly, precisely, as if re-*

porting to an employer] Six thirteen P.M. Mr. Faulkner leaves home on Long Island. Wears formal dress suit. Drives car himself, alone. Special notation: Unusual speed all the way to New York.

FLINT: Where does Mr. Faulkner go?

VAN FLEET: He drives up to the Faulkner Building and goes in. It is now seven fifty-seven P.M., all offices closed. I wait outside, in my car. Nine thirty-five P.M. Mr. Faulkner comes out with Miss Andre. Miss Andre is dressed formally. Special notation: Miss Andre is wearing a corsage of orchids of unusual proportions. They drive away.

FLINT: Where do they go?

VAN FLEET: No one is perfect in this world.

FLINT: What do you mean?

VAN FLEET: I mean I lost track of them. Due to Mr. Faulkner's speed and to an accident.

FLINT: What accident?

VAN FLEET: My left fender crashing into a truck; damages for which fender charged to Mrs. Faulkner.

FLINT: What did you do when you lost track of them?

VAN FLEET: Returned to the Faulkner Building and waited.

FLINT: When did they return?

VAN FLEET: Ten thirty P.M. exactly. A gray car follows them. Mr. Faulkner gets out and helps

Miss Andre. While she rings the bell, he opens the door of the gray car; a tall gentleman in formal clothes steps out, and together they help out a third gentleman, the latter wearing a dark gray sport coat. Special notation: The aforementioned gentleman shows signs of inebriation. They all go into the Faulkner Building.

FLINT: Then what did you do?

VAN FLEET: Left my car and went into Gary's Grill, across the street from the Faulkner Building. I must explain that I allow myself time to take nourishment every four hours while on duty and four hours had elapsed since we left Long Island. I sat at a window and watched the Faulkner entrance door.

FLINT: What did you observe?

VAN FLEET: Nothing—for fifteen minutes. Then the man in the gray coat comes out and starts the car—the gray car. Obviously in a hurry. Drives south.

FLINT: Did you see the other stranger leave?

VAN FLEET: Yes, ten minutes later. He gets into a car which stands at the curb. I don't know how it got there, but there it is and he seems to have the keys, for he gets in and drives away. South.

FLINT: Have you ever seen Mr. Faulkner with these two men before?

VAN FLEET: No. First time I ever saw them.

FLINT: What did you do when they left?

VAN FLEET: I wait. Mr. Faulkner is now alone up

in the penthouse with Miss Andre. I'm curious—
professionally. Decide to do some closer investi-
gating. Have a special observation post; had
used it before.

FLINT: And where is that?

VAN FLEET: At the Sky Top. Night club, roof of
Brooks Building, three doors from Faulkner's.
There's an open gallery there, off the dance
floor. You go out and you can see the Faulkner
penthouse clear as the palm of your hand. I go
out, I look and I yell.

FLINT: What do you see?

VAN FLEET: No lights. Karen Andre's white gown
shimmering in the moonlight. She is hoisting a
man's body up on the parapet. A man in evening clothes. Faulkner. He's unconscious. No
resistance. She pushes him with all her strength.
He goes over the parapet. Down. Into space.

FLINT: Then what do you do?

VAN FLEET: I rush back into the dining room.
Yell about what I'd seen. A crowd follows me
down to the Faulkner Building. We find the
bloody mess on the pavement and Miss Andre
sobbing over it, fit to move a first-night audience.

FLINT: Did you speak to her?

VAN FLEET: No. The police arrive and I report
what I'd seen, as I've told you here.

FLINT: Your witness.

[STEVENS *gets up and walks slowly toward* VAN
FLEET, *eyeing him steadily*]

STEVENS: Can you kindly tell us, Mr. Van Fleet, when did you start in the employ of Mrs. Faulkner?

VAN FLEET: October thirteenth last.

STEVENS: Can you tell us the date of Mr. and Mrs. Faulkner's wedding?

VAN FLEET: October twelfth. The day before.

STEVENS: Exactly. *Just the day before*. In other words, Mrs. Faulkner hired you to spy on her husband the day after their wedding?

VAN FLEET: So it seems.

STEVENS: What were Mrs. Faulkner's instructions when you were hired?

VAN FLEET: To watch every action of Mr. Faulkner and report in detail.

STEVENS: Any special attention to Miss Andre?

VAN FLEET: Not specified.

STEVENS: Had Mr. Faulkner been calling on Miss Andre after his marriage?

VAN FLEET: Yes. Frequently.

STEVENS: In the daytime?

VAN FLEET: Seldom.

STEVENS: Did you report that to Mrs. Faulkner?

VAN FLEET: I did.

STEVENS: What was Mrs. Faulkner's reaction to these reports?

VAN FLEET: Mrs. Faulkner is a lady and, as such, she has no reactions.

STEVENS: Did she seem worried?

VAN FLEET: I don't believe so.
[*He declaims in a slightly unnatural manner*]
Mr. Faulkner was the most devoted of husbands
and he loved his wife dearly.

STEVENS: Just how do you know that?

VAN FLEET: Those are Mrs. Faulkner's own words.

STEVENS: Now, Mr. Van Fleet, can you tell us
exactly what time you started for the Sky Top
Night Club on the evening of January sixteenth?

VAN FLEET: At eleven thirty-two exactly.

STEVENS: How long a walk is it from the Faulkner
Building to the Sky Top?

VAN FLEET: Three minutes.

STEVENS: What time was it when you came out
to the balcony at the Sky Top?

VAN FLEET: Eleven fifty-seven.

STEVENS: So it took you exactly twenty-five minutes to get to the balcony. What were you doing
the rest of the time?

VAN FLEET: Of course, they have a dance floor at
the Sky Top . . . and other things.

STEVENS: Did you take advantage of the . . . "other
things"?

VAN FLEET: Well, I just had a couple of drinks, if
I understand the drift of your curiosity. But it
doesn't mean that you can say I was intox-
icated.

STEVENS: I have said nothing of the kind—as yet. Now, then, you saw Miss Andre pushing Mr. Faulkner off the roof, and it was a little distance away, in the darkness, and you were . . . well, shall we say you just had a couple of drinks?

VAN FLEET: The drinks had nothing to do with it.

STEVENS: Are you quite certain that she was *pushing* him? Isn't it possible that she was *struggling* with him?

VAN FLEET: Well, it's a funny way of struggling. If I were struggling with a man, I wouldn't be hoisting him up by his . . . I wouldn't be hoisting him up, I mean.

STEVENS: Mr. Van Fleet, what were Mrs. Faulkner's instructions to you before you came here to testify?

VAN FLEET: [*With indignation*] I received no instructions of any kind. I may inform you that Mrs. Faulkner is not here to instruct me, were she inclined to do so. She has been taken to California by her father—to rest her shattered nerves.

STEVENS: Mr. Van Fleet, do you think that Mr. Faulkner's suicide is very flattering to Mrs. Faulkner?

FLINT: We object!

JUDGE HEATH: Objection sustained.

STEVENS: Mr. Van Fleet, can you tell us how much

a witness to Mr. Faulkner's *murder* would be worth to Mrs. Faulkner?

FLINT: [*Jumping up*] We object, your Honor!

JUDGE HEATH: Objection sustained.

VAN FLEET: I should like to remind Mr. Stevens that he may be sued for making insinuations such as these.

STEVENS: I made no insinuation, Mr. Van Fleet. I merely asked a question in a general way.

VAN FLEET: Well, I would like to inform you—in a general way—that perjury is not part of a private investigator's duties.

STEVENS: No special notations to the rule?

VAN FLEET: None!

STEVENS: That is all, Mr. Van Fleet.

KAREN: Not quite. I want you to ask him two more questions, Stevens.

STEVENS: Certainly, Miss Andre. What are the questions?

[KAREN *whispers to* STEVENS; *he is astonished*]

STEVENS: What kind of a car do you drive, Mr. Van Fleet?

VAN FLEET: [*Astonished, too*] A brown Buick two-door sedan. Last year's model. Old but serviceable.

[KAREN *whispers to* STEVENS]

STEVENS: Did you see any car following the gentleman in the gray coat when he drove away, Mr. Van Fleet?

VAN FLEET: I cannot recall that I did. The traffic was quite heavy at that time.

STEVENS: That's all, Mr. Van Fleet.

[VAN FLEET *exits*]

FLINT: Inspector Sweeney!

CLERK: Inspector Sweeney!

[POLICE INSPECTOR SWEENEY, *round-faced, somewhat naive, walks to the stand*]

CLERK: You solemnly swear to tell the truth, the whole truth and nothing but the truth so help you God?

SWEENEY: I do.

FLINT: Your name?

SWEENEY: Elmer Sweeney.

FLINT: Your occupation?

SWEENEY: Inspector of Police.

FLINT: On the night of January sixteenth were you called upon to investigate Bjorn Faulkner's death?

SWEENEY: Yes, sir. I was one of the first officers to reach the spot.

FLINT: Did you question Miss Andre?

SWEENEY: Not right away. Before I could do anything, that fellow Van Fleet rushed up to me and yelled that he had seen Karen Andre throw Faulkner off the roof.

FLINT: How did Miss Andre react to this?

SWEENEY: She was stunned. She stood there, her eyes wide fit to burst. And then, cross my heart, sir, she started laughing. I thought she'd went crazy.

FLINT: What did you do?

SWEENEY: I ordered her held for questioning and we took her up with us in the elevator—to examine the penthouse. What a joint!

FLINT: Did you find anything unusual?

SWEENEY: Unusual—yes, sir. The bedroom.

FLINT: Ah, and what did you find in the bedroom?

SWEENEY: Nightgowns, sir. Lace nightgowns, just about made of thin air. A crystal bathtub in the bathroom. And we turned the shower on— and the water was perfumed.

FLINT: [*Smiling*] You misunderstood my question, Inspector. I wasn't referring to the esthetic values of the penthouse. I asked if you found anything unusual that could be connected with Bjorn Faulkner's death?

SWEENEY: Yes, sir. In the living room.

FLINT: And what was that?

SWEENEY: A letter. It was lying in plain sight on a table. It was sealed and the address said: "To whomsoever finds it first."
[FLINT *takes a letter from the* CLERK *and hands it to* SWEENEY]

FLINT: Is this the letter?

SWEENEY: Yes, sir.

FLINT: Will you kindly read it to the jury?

SWEENEY: [*Reading*] "If any future historian wants to record my last advice to humanity, I'll say that I found only two enjoyable things on this earth whose every door was open to me: My whip over the world and Karen Andre. To those who can use it, the advice is worth what it has cost mankind. Bjorn Faulkner."

FLINT: [*Handing letter to* CLERK] Submitted as evidence.

JUDGE HEATH: Accepted as Exhibit A.

FLINT: Did you question Miss Andre about this letter?

SWEENEY: I did. She said that Faulkner wrote the letter and left it there, on the table, and ordered her not to touch it, then went out to the roof garden. She struggled with him, when she saw what he was going to do, but she couldn't stop him.

FLINT: Did you ask her who had been with them that night?

SWEENEY: I did. She said two gentlemen had: they were friends of Mr. Faulkner and *she had never seen them before*. He picked them up in a night club, that evening, and brought them along. She said their names were "Jerry White" and "Dick Saunders."

FLINT: Did you try to find any gentlemen by these names among Mr. Faulkner's acquaintances?

SWEENEY: We did. We found that no one had ever heard of them.

FLINT: And Miss Andre told you, as she did at the

inquest, that she had never seen these two men before?

SWEENEY: Yes, sir.

FLINT: Was she very emphatic about that?

SWEENEY: Yes, sir. *Very*.

FLINT: That is all, Inspector.

STEVENS: Miss Andre told you that she had struggled with Faulkner to prevent his suicide. Did you notice any evidence of a struggle in her clothes?

SWEENEY: Yes, sir. Her dress was torn. It had diamond shoulder straps, and one of them was broken, so that she had to hold the dress up with one hand.

STEVENS: What did you think of that?

SWEENEY: [*Embarrassed*] Do I have to answer?

STEVENS: You certainly do.

SWEENEY: Well . . . I wished he had broken the other strap, too.

STEVENS: I meant, did you think that the dress looked as though it had been torn in a struggle?

SWEENEY: It looked like it, yes, sir.

STEVENS: Now, can you tell us why on earth you turned the shower on in the bathroom?

SWEENEY: [*Embarrassed*] Well, you see, we heard Faulkner had wine instead of water in it.

STEVENS: [*Laughing*] You mustn't believe all the

legends you hear about Bjorn Faulkner . . . That's all, Inspector.

[SWEENEY *leaves the stand and exits*]

FLINT: Magda Svenson!

CLERK: Magda Svenson!

[MAGDA SVENSON *enters and waddles toward the witness stand. She is fat, middle-aged, with tight, drawn lips, suspicious eyes, an air of offended righteousness. Her clothes are plain, old-fashioned, meticulously neat*]

You solemnly swear to tell the truth, the whole truth and nothing but the truth so help you God?

MAGDA: [*Speaks with a pronounced Swedish accent*] I swear. [*She takes the Bible, raises it slowly to her lips, kisses it solemnly, and hands it back, taking the whole ceremony with a profound religious seriousness*]

FLINT: What is your name?

MAGDA: You know it. You just call me.

FLINT: Kindly answer my questions without argument. State your name.

MAGDA: Magda Svenson.

FLINT: What is your occupation?

MAGDA: I am housekeeper.

FLINT: By whom were you employed last?

MAGDA: By Herr Bjorn Faulkner and before that his father.

FLINT: How long have you been employed by them?

MAGDA: I been in the family thirty-eight years. I remember Herr Bjorn since he was little child.

FLINT: When did you come to America?

MAGDA: I been here five years.

FLINT: What were the duties Mr. Faulkner assigned to you?

MAGDA: I keep penthouse for him. He visit here every year or so. I stay even after he go, when he get married. But I never employed by this one.

[*She points at* KAREN *with undisguised hatred*]

FLINT: Now, Mrs. Svenson, what—

MAGDA: [*Offended*] *Miss* Svenson.

FLINT: I beg your pardon, Miss Svenson. What do you know about Miss Andre's relations with Mr. Faulkner?

MAGDA: [*With forceful indignation*] Decent woman like me shouldn't know about such things. But sin is shameless in this world.

FLINT: Tell us about it, Miss Svenson.

MAGDA: From very first day this woman appeared, she was sleeping with Herr Faulkner. It isn't good thing when a man forgets line between his bed and his desk. And she put her claws tight on both. Sometimes, they talked loans and dividends in bed; other times, the door to his office was locked and, under the window shades that was pulled down, I seen her lace pants on the window sill.

STEVENS: [*Jumping up*] Your Honor! We object!

FLINT: I think Miss Andre should have objected many years ago!

STEVENS: Such line of testimony is outrageous!

FLINT: These are facts pertaining to the vital question of their relationship and—

JUDGE HEATH: [*Rapping his gavel*] Silence, gentlemen! I shall ask the witness to word her testimony more carefully.

MAGDA: Sin is sin any name you call it, Judge.

FLINT: Miss Svenson, do you know of any instance when Miss Andre's conduct was detrimental to Mr. Faulkner in other ways than moral?

MAGDA: I do so. You try count up all money he waste on that woman.

FLINT: Can you tell us an instance of Mr. Faulkner's extravagance?

MAGDA: I tell you. He had a platinum gown made for her. Yes, I said platinum. Fine mesh, fine and soft as silk. She wore it on her naked body. He would make a fire in the fireplace and he would heat the dress and then put it on her. It cooled and you could see her body in silver sheen, and it been more decent if she had been naked. And she ask to put it on as hot as she can stand, and if it burned her shameless skin, she laughed like the pagan she is, and he kissed the burn, wild like tiger!

STEVENS: Your Honor! We object! This testimony is irrelevant and only tends to prejudice the jury against Miss Andre!

KAREN: [*Very calmly*] Let her talk, Stevens.
[*She looks at the jury and for a swift moment we see a smile, mischievous, tempting, radiant, a surprise in this cold business woman, revealing an entirely different type of femininity*]
Perhaps it may prejudice the jury in my favor.

[*Commotion in the courtroom.* STEVENS *stares at* KAREN. JUDGE HEATH *strikes his gavel*]

FLINT: Mr. Stevens has my sympathy. His client is not an easy one to handle.

JUDGE HEATH: Silence! Objection overruled.

FLINT: Did you observe Mr. Faulkner's attitude toward his marriage?

MAGDA: He was happy for first time in his life. He was happy like decent man what found right road.

FLINT: Did you know of anything that made him worry in those days, that could bring him to suicide eventually?

MAGDA: No. Nothing.

FLINT: Now, tell us, Miss Svenson, did you observe Miss Andre's attitude toward Mr. Faulkner's marriage?

MAGDA: She silent, like stone statue. She—

[*There is a commotion in the courtroom.* NANCY LEE FAULKNER *appears at the spectators'*

door at left. NANCY LEE FAULKNER *is twenty-
two, blonde, slender, delicate, perfect as a costly porcelain statuette. Her exquisite white skin
is a contrast to the somber, unrelieved black of
her clothes; they are clothes of mourning,
severe and in perfect taste.* EVERYONE *in the
courtroom stares at her.* KAREN *turns toward
her slowly. But* NANCY LEE *does not look at*
KAREN. FLINT *cannot restrain an exclamation of
astonishment*]

FLINT: Mrs. Faulkner!

NANCY LEE: [*She speaks in a soft, slow voice*] I
understand you wanted to call me as a witness,
Mr. Flint?

FLINT: I did, Mrs. Faulkner, but I thought you
were in California.

NANCY LEE: I was. I escaped.

FLINT: You escaped?

NANCY LEE: Father was concerned over my health.
He wouldn't allow me to come back. But I
want to do my duty toward the memory of . . .
[*Her voice trembles a little*]
my husband. I'm at your disposal, Mr. Flint.

FLINT: I can only express my deepest appreciation,
Mrs. Faulkner. If you will kindly take a seat, we
will be ready for you in just a little while.

NANCY LEE: Thank you.
[*She takes one of the spectators' chairs at the
wall, at right*]

FLINT: [*To* MAGDA] You were telling us about

Miss Andre's attitude toward Mr. Faulkner's marriage, Miss Svenson.

MAGDA: I said she keep silent. But I hear her crying one night, after marriage. Crying, sobbing— and that the first and only time in her life.

FLINT: Did she seem to . . . suffer much?

MAGDA: Suffer? No. Not her. One man more or less make no much difference to her. I seen her unfaithful to Herr Faulkner on the night of his wedding.

[*Reaction in the courtroom. Even* KAREN *takes notice, a little startled*]

FLINT: Unfaithful? With whom?

MAGDA: I don't know the man. I seen him first time the night of Herr Faulkner's wedding.

FLINT: Tell us about it.

MAGDA: I gone to wedding. Ah, it was beautiful. My poor Herr Bjorn so handsome and the young bride all white and lovely as lily.
[*Sniffles audibly*]
I cried like looking at my own children.
[*Her voice changes; she points at* KAREN *ferociously*]
But *she* not go to wedding!

FLINT: Did Miss Andre stay at home?

MAGDA: She stay home. I come back early. I come in servants' door. She not hear me come. She was home. But she was not alone.

FLINT: Who was with her?

MAGDA: *He* was. The man. Out on the roof, in the

garden. It was dark, but I could see. He holding her in his arms and I think he want to crush her bones. He bent her back so far I think she fall into her reflection in the pool. And then he kiss her and I think he never get his lips off hers.

FLINT: And then?

MAGDA: She step aside and say something. I cannot hear, she speak very soft. He not say word. He just take her hand and kiss it and hold it on his lips so long I get tired waiting and go back to my room.

FLINT: Did you learn the name of that man?

MAGDA: No.

FLINT: Did you see him again?

MAGDA: Yes. Once.

FLINT: And when was that?

MAGDA: The night of January sixteenth.

[*A movement in the courtroom*]

FLINT: Tell us about it, Miss Svenson.

MAGDA: Well, *she* very strange that day. She call me and said I have the rest of day off. And I been suspicious.

FLINT: Why did that make you suspicious?

MAGDA: My day off is Thursday and I not asked for second day. So I said I not need day off, and she said she not need me. So I go.

FLINT: What time did you go?

MAGDA: About four o'clock. But I want to know secret. I come back.

FLINT: When did you come back?

MAGDA: About ten at night. The house dark, she not home. So I wait. Half hour after, I hear them come. I seen Herr Faulkner with her. So I afraid to stay. But before I go I seen two gentlemen with them. One gentleman, he drunk, I not know him.

FLINT: Did you know the other one?

MAGDA: The other one—he was tall and lanky and had sharp cheekbones. He was the man I seen kissing Miss Andre.

FLINT: [*Almost triumphant*] That's all, Miss Svenson.

[MAGDA *is about to leave the stand.* STEVENS *stops her*]

STEVENS: Just a minute, Miss Svenson. You still have to have a little talk with me.

MAGDA: [*Resentfully*] For what? I say all I know.

STEVENS: You may know the answers to a few more questions. Now, you said that you had seen that stranger kissing Miss Andre?

MAGDA: Yes, I did.

STEVENS: You said it was dark, that night when you saw him for the first time?

MAGDA: Yes, it was dark.

STEVENS: And, on the night of January sixteenth, when you were so ingeniously spying on your mistress, you said that you saw her come in with Mr. Faulkner, and you hurried to depart in order not to be caught. Am I correct?

MAGDA: You have a good memory.

STEVENS: You just had a swift glance at the two gentlemen with them?

MAGDA: Yes.

STEVENS: Can you tell us what the drunken gentleman looked like?

MAGDA: How can I? No time to notice face and too dark at door.

STEVENS: So! It was too dark? And you were in a hurry? And yet you were able to identify a man you had seen but once before?

MAGDA: [*With all the strength of her righteous indignation*] Let me tell you, mister! I'm under oath as you say, and I'm religious woman and respect oath. But I said it was the same man and I say it again!

STEVENS: That it all. Thank you, Miss Svenson.

[MAGDA *leaves the stand, carefully avoiding looking at* KAREN. *There is a little hush of expectancy as all eyes turn to* NANCY LEE FAULKNER. FLINT *calls solemnly, distinctly*]

FLINT: Mrs. Faulkner!

[NANCY LEE *rises and walks to the stand slowly, as if each step taxed her strength. She is calm, but gives the impression that the ordeal is painful to her and that she is making a brave effort to do her duty*]

CLERK: You solemnly swear to tell the truth, the

whole truth and nothing but the truth so help
you God?

NANCY LEE: I do.

FLINT: What is your name?

NANCY LEE: Nancy Lee Faulkner.

FLINT: What relation were you to the late Bjorn
Faulkner?

NANCY LEE: I was . . . his wife.

FLINT: I realize how painful this is to you, Mrs.
Faulkner, and I appreciate your courage, but I
will have to ask you many questions that will
awaken sad memories.

NANCY LEE: I am ready, Mr. Flint.

FLINT: When did you first meet Bjorn Faulkner?

NANCY LEE: In August of last year.

FLINT: Where did you meet him?

NANCY LEE: At a ball given by my friend Sandra
van Renssler, in Newport.

FLINT: Will you kindly tell us about it, Mrs.
Faulkner?

NANCY LEE: Sandra introduced us. I remember she
said: "Here's a tough one for you, Nancy. I
wonder whether you'll add *this* scalp to the
well-known collection." Sandra had always insisted on exaggerating my popularity . . . I
danced with him, that night. We danced in the
garden, under the trees, and stopped on the
edge of a pool. We were alone in the darkness,
with the faint sound of the Blue Danube Waltz

filling the silence. Mr. Faulkner reached up to pick a rose for me. As he tore it off, his hand brushed my bare shoulder. I don't know why, but I blushed. He noticed it and apologized, graciously, smiling. Then he took me back to the guests . . . I think we both felt a silent understanding, that night, for we did not dance again with each other.

FLINT: When did you see Mr. Faulkner again?

NANCY LEE: Three days later. I invited him to dine at my home on Long Island. It was a real Swedish meal—and I cooked it myself.

FLINT: Did you see him often after that?

NANCY LEE: Yes, quite often. His visits became more and more frequent until the day . . .

[*Her voice breaks*]

FLINT: Until the day?

NANCY LEE: [*Her voice barely above a whisper*] The day he proposed to me.

FLINT: Please tell us about it, Mrs. Faulkner.

NANCY LEE: We went driving, Mr. Faulkner and I, alone. It was a beautiful day, with a bright, cold sunshine. I was driving my car—and I felt so young, so happy that I grew reckless. I . . .
[*Her voice trembles; she is silent for a few seconds, as if fighting the pain of these memories, then resumes with a faint smile of apology*]
I'm sorry. It's a little . . . hard for me to think of . . . those days . . . I was reckless . . . reckless enough to lose my way. We stopped on a

strange country road. I laughed and said:
"We're lost. I've kidnapped you and I won't
release you." He answered: "The ransom you
want is not in circulation." Then, suddenly, he
seized my hand and looking straight at me,
said: "What's the use of pretending? I love you,
Nancy..."
[*Her voice breaks into a sob. She buries her face
in a lace handkerchief*]

FLINT: I'm so sorry, Mrs. Faulkner. If you wish to
be dismissed now and continue tomorrow—

NANCY LEE: [*Raising her head*] Thank you, I'm
all right. I can go on ... It was then that I first
learned about the desperate state of Mr. Faulkner's fortune. He said that he had to tell me the
truth, that he could not ask me to marry him
when he had nothing to offer me. But I ... I
loved him. So I told him that money had never
meant anything to me.

FLINT: Did Mr. Faulkner feel hopeless about the
future, when your engagement was announced?

NANCY LEE: No, not at all. He said that my faith
in him and my courage helped him so much. I
told him that it was our duty to save his enterprises, our duty to the world he had wronged,
not to ourselves. I made him realize his past
mistakes and he was ready to atone for them.
We were entering a new life together, a life of
unselfish devotion to the service and welfare of
others.

FLINT: Did you remain in New York after your
wedding?

NANCY LEE: Yes. We made our home in my Long

Island residence. Mr. Faulkner gave up his New York penthouse.

FLINT: Did Mr. Faulkner tell you of his relations with Miss Andre?

NANCY LEE: No, not then. But he did, two weeks after our wedding. He came to me and said: "Dearest, there is a woman—there *was* a woman—and I feel I must tell you about her." I said: "I know it. You don't have to say a word if you'd rather not, dear."

FLINT: And what did Mr. Faulkner tell you?

NANCY LEE: He said: "Karen Andre is the cause and the symbol of my darkest years. I am going to dismiss her."

FLINT: What did you answer?

NANCY LEE: I said that I understood him and that he was right. "But," I said, "we must not be cruel. Perhaps you can find another position for Miss Andre." He said that he'd provide for her financially, but that he never wanted to see her again.

FLINT: He, therefore, dismissed Miss Andre voluntarily, of his own choice?

NANCY LEE: [*Proudly*] Mr. Flint, there are two kinds of women in this world. And *my* kind is never jealous of . . . the other.

FLINT: What was Mr. Faulkner's business situation after your marriage?

NANCY LEE: I'm afraid I don't understand much about business. But I know that Father made a loan—a very large loan—to my husband.

FLINT: Mrs. Faulkner, will you tell us whether you think it possible that your husband had any reason to commit suicide?

NANCY LEE: I think it totally impossible.

FLINT: Did he ever speak of his plans for the future?

NANCY LEE: We used to dream of the future, together. Even . . . even on the evening before his . . . his death. We were sitting by the fire, in his study, talking about the years ahead. We knew that we would not be wealthy for a long time, if ever. But we didn't care about that. We had renounced material concerns, with all their consequences: pride, selfishness, ambition, the desire to rise above our fellow-men. We wanted to devote our life to spiritual values. We were planning to leave the city, to be part of some modest community, to be like everyone else.

FLINT: And this was on the night of January fifteenth, the day before his death?

NANCY LEE: [Feebly] Yes.

FLINT: What did Mr. Faulkner do on the day of January sixteenth?

NANCY LEE: He spent it in town, on business, as usual. He came home late in the afternoon. He said that he had to attend a business banquet in New York that night, so he did not have dinner at home. He left at about six o'clock.

FLINT: What banquet was Mr. Faulkner supposed to attend?

NANCY LEE: He did not tell me and I didn't ask. I made it a point never to interfere with his business.

FLINT: Did you notice anything peculiar when he said goodbye to you, that night?

NANCY LEE: No, not a thing. He kissed me and said that he'd try to come home early. I stood at the door and watched him drive away. He waved to me as his car disappeared in the dusk. I stood there for a few minutes, thinking of how happy we were, of what a perfect dream our love had been, like a delicate idyll, like . . . [*Her voice trembles*] I didn't know that our beautiful romance would . . . indirectly . . . through jealousy . . . bring about his . . . his death. [*She drops her head, hiding her face in her hands, sobbing audibly, as* STEVENS's *voice booms out*]

STEVENS: Your Honor! We object! Move that that be stricken out!

JUDGE HEATH: The witness's last sentence may go out.

FLINT: Thank you, Mrs. Faulkner. That is all.

STEVENS: [*Coldly*] Will you be able to answer a few questions now, Mrs. Faulkner?

NANCY LEE: [*Raising her tear-stained face, proudly*] As many as you wish, Mr. Stevens.

STEVENS: [*Softly*] You said that your romance was like a perfect dream, didn't you?

NANCY LEE: Yes.

STEVENS: A sacred troth that regenerated a soul?

NANCY LEE: Yes.

STEVENS: A beautiful, uplifting relationship based on *mutual trust?*

NANCY LEE: [*Becoming a little astonished*] Yes.

STEVENS: [*Changing his voice, fiercely*] Then why did you hire a detective to spy on your husband?

NANCY LEE: [*A little flustered*] I ... that is ... I didn't hire a detective to spy on my husband. I hired him to protect Mr. Faulkner.

STEVENS: Will you kindly explain that?

NANCY LEE: Well ... you see ... you see, some time ago, Mr. Faulkner had been threatened by a gangster—"Guts" Regan. I believe they call him that. Mr. Faulkner did not pay any attention to it—no one could intimidate him—and he refused to hire a bodyguard. But I was worried ... so as soon as we were married, I hired Mr. Van Fleet to watch him. I did it secretly, because I knew that Mr. Faulkner would object.

STEVENS: How could a sleuth following at a distance protect Mr. Faulkner?

NANCY LEE: Well, I heard that the underworld has a way of finding out those things and I thought they would not attack a man who was constantly watched.

STEVENS: So all Mr. Van Fleet had to do was to watch Mr. Faulkner?

NANCY LEE: Yes.

STEVENS: Mr. Faulkner alone?

NANCY LEE: Yes.

STEVENS: Not Mr. Faulkner *and* Miss Andre?

NANCY LEE: Mr. Stevens, that supposition is insulting to me.

STEVENS: I haven't noticed *you* sparing insults, Mrs. Faulkner.

NANCY LEE: I'm sorry, Mr. Stevens. I assure you that was not my intention.

STEVENS: You said that Mr. Faulkner told you he never wanted to see Miss Andre again?

NANCY LEE: Yes, he did.

STEVENS: And yet, he called on her after his marriage, he called on her often and *at night*. Your detective told you that, didn't he?

NANCY LEE: Yes. I knew it.

STEVENS: How do you explain it?

NANCY LEE: I cannot explain it. How can I know what blackmail she was holding over his head?

STEVENS: How do you explain the fact that Mr. Faulkner lied to you about the business banquet on the night of January sixteenth and went directly to Miss Andre's house?

NANCY LEE: If I could explain that, Mr. Stevens, I might be able to save you the bother of this trial. We would have an explanation of my husband's mysterious death. All I know is that she made him come to her house for some reason which he could not tell me—and that he was found dead, that night.

STEVENS: Mrs. Faulkner, I want you to answer one more question.

NANCY LEE: Yes?

STEVENS: I want you to state here, under oath, that Bjorn Faulkner loved you.

NANCY LEE: Bjorn Faulkner was mine.

STEVENS: That is all, Mrs. Faulkner.

KAREN: [*Calmly, distinctly*] No. That's not all.

[*All eyes turn to her*]

Ask her one more question, Stevens.

STEVENS: What is it, Miss Andre?

KAREN: Ask her whether she loved him.

NANCY LEE: [*Sitting straight up, with the icy poise of a perfect lady*] I did, Miss Andre.

KAREN: [*Jumping to her feet*] Then how can you speak of *him* as you did? How can you sit here and lie, lie about him, when he can't come back to defend himself?

[*JUDGE HEATH strikes his gavel violently. NANCY LEE gasps and jumps to her feet*]

NANCY LEE: I won't stand for it! Why should I be questioned by . . . by the murderess of my husband!

[*She falls back on the chair, sobbing. FLINT rushes to her*]

KAREN: [*Calmly*] That's all.

FLINT: I'm so sorry, Mrs. Faulkner!

JUDGE HEATH: The court will now adjourn till ten o'clock tomorrow morning.

[*EVERYONE rises. JUDGE HEATH leaves the courtroom, while FLINT helps NANCY LEE down from the witness stand. As she passes by* KAREN, NANCY LEE *throws a defiant look at her.* KAREN *stands straight and says aloud, so that all heads turn to her]*

KAREN: One of us is lying. And we both know which one!

CURTAIN

Act Two

SCENE: *Same scene as at the opening of Act I.* KAREN *is sitting at the defense table, as proudly calm as ever. When the curtain rises, the* BAILIFF *raps.*

BAILIFF: Court attention!

[JUDGE HEATH *enters.* EVERYONE *rises*]

Superior Court Number Eleven of the State of New York. The Honorable Judge William Heath presiding.

[JUDGE HEATH *sits down,* BAILIFF *raps, and* EVERYONE *resumes his seat*]

JUDGE HEATH: The people of the State of New York versus Karen Andre.

FLINT: Ready, your Honor.

STEVENS: Ready, your Honor.

JUDGE HEATH: The District Attorney may proceed.

FLINT: If your Honor please, the prosecution has

67

one more witness to introduce. Mr. John Graham Whitfield!

CLERK: John Graham Whitfield!

[MR. WHITFIELD *comes in, followed by* NANCY LEE. MR. WHITFIELD *is tall, gray-haired, perfectly groomed, a thorough gentleman with the imperious manner of a wartime generalissimo.* NANCY LEE *walks in slowly, head downcast.* WHITFIELD *pats her hand affectionately as if to encourage her, as they part; he walks to the witness stand, and she takes a chair at right*]

CLERK: You solemnly swear to tell the truth, the whole truth and nothing but the truth so help you God?

WHITFIELD: I do.

FLINT: What is your name?

WHITFIELD: John Graham Whitfield.

FLINT: What is your occupation?

WHITFIELD: I am president of the Whitfield National Bank.

FLINT: Were you related to the late Bjorn Faulkner?

WHITFIELD: I was his father-in-law.

FLINT: It is obvious, Mr. Whitfield, that you are well qualified to pass judgment on financial matters. Can you tell us about the state of Mr. Faulkner's business at the time preceding his death?

WHITFIELD: I shall say it was desperate, but not hopeless. My bank made a loan of twenty-five million dollars to Mr. Faulkner in an effort to save his enterprises. Needless to say, that money is lost.

FLINT: What prompted you to make that loan, Mr. Whitfield?

WHITFIELD: He was the husband of my only daughter; her happiness has always been paramount to me. But my motives were not entirely personal: realizing the countless tragedies of small investors that the crash would bring, I considered it my duty to make every possible effort to prevent it.

FLINT: Is it possible that you would have risked such a considerable sum in Mr. Faulkner's enterprises if you believed them hopelessly destined to crash?

WHITFIELD: Certainly not. It was a difficult undertaking, but I had full confidence that my business acumen would have prevented the crash— had Faulkner lived.

FLINT: He, therefore, had no reason to commit suicide as far as his business affairs were concerned?

WHITFIELD: He had every reason for remaining alive.

FLINT: Now, Mr. Whitfield, can you tell us whether Mr. Faulkner was happy in his family life, in his relations with your daughter?

WHITFIELD: Mr. Flint, I would like to state that I have always regarded the home and the family as the most important institutions in our lives. You, therefore, will believe me when I tell you how important my daughter's family happiness was to me—and she had found perfect happiness with Mr. Faulkner.

FLINT: Mr. Whitfield, what was your opinion of Mr. Faulkner?

WHITFIELD: It is only fair to admit that he had many qualities of which I did not approve. We were as different as two human beings could be: I believe in one's duty above all; Bjorn Faulkner believed in nothing but his own pleasure.

FLINT: From your knowledge of him, Mr. Whitfield, would you say you consider it possible that Mr. Faulkner committed suicide?

WHITFIELD: I consider it absolutely impossible.

FLINT: Thank you, Mr. Whitfield. That is all.

STEVENS: Mr. Whitfield, were you very fond of your son-in-law?

WHITFIELD: Yes.

STEVENS: And you never disagreed with him, never lost your temper in a quarrel?

WHITFIELD: [*With a tolerant, superior smile*] Mr. Stevens, I never lose my temper.

STEVENS: If my memory serves me right, there was some kind of trouble at the time you made that stupendous loan to Mr. Faulkner. Wasn't there something said to the effect that you denied making the loan?

WHITFIELD: Purely a misunderstanding, I assure you. I must admit that Mr. Faulkner made a . . . somewhat unethical attempt to hasten that

loan, which was quite unnecessary, since I granted it gladly—for my daughter's sake.

STEVENS: You said that your fortune has been
badly damaged by the Faulkner crash?

WHITFIELD: Yes.

STEVENS: And your financial situation is rather
strained at present?

WHITFIELD: Yes.

STEVENS: Then how could you afford to offer a one
hundred thousand dollar reward for the arrest
and conviction of "Guts" Regan?

FLINT: Objection! What has that got to do with
the case?

WHITFIELD: Your Honor, I would like to have the
privilege of explaining this.

JUDGE HEATH: Very well.

WHITFIELD: I did offer such a reward. I was
prompted by a feeling of civic duty. The gentleman commonly known as "Guts" Regan is a
notorious criminal. I offered that reward for
evidence that would make his arrest and conviction possible. However, I agree with Mr. Flint
that this has nothing to do with the present
case.

STEVENS: Mr. Whitfield, can you tell us why you
left for California in such a hurry before the
beginning of this trial?

WHITFIELD: I think the answer is obvious. My
daughter was crushed by the sudden tragedy. I

hastened to take her away, to save her health, perhaps her life.

STEVENS: You love your daughter profoundly?

WHITFIELD: Yes.

STEVENS: You have always made it a point that her every wish should be granted?

WHITFIELD: I can proudly say yes.

STEVENS: When she—or you—desire anything, you don't stop at the price, do you?

WHITFIELD: We don't have to.

STEVENS: Then would you refuse to buy her the man she wanted?

FLINT: Your Honor! We—

WHITFIELD: Mr. Stevens!

STEVENS: You wouldn't stop if it took your entire fortune to break the first unbreakable man you'd ever met?

FLINT: Your Honor! We object!

JUDGE HEATH: Sustained.

STEVENS: Now, Mr. Whitfield, are you going to tell us that your money had nothing to do with Mr. Faulkner dismissing Miss Andre? That no ultimatum was delivered to him?

WHITFIELD: [*His tone is slightly less kindly and composed than before*] You are quite mistaken in your insinuations. My daughter was no more jealous of Miss Andre than she would be of Mr. Faulkner's soiled underwear. All men have some at one time or another!

STEVENS: I'd be careful of statements such as these, Mr. Whitfield. Remember that your daughter paid for what Karen Andre got free!

FLINT: Your Honor! We—

[WHITFIELD *jumps to his feet; his face is distorted; he is shaking with fury.* JUDGE HEATH *raps his gavel, but to no avail.* NANCY LEE *jumps up, crying hysterically through* WHITFIELD'S *speech*]

NANCY LEE: Father! Father!

WHITFIELD: Why you . . . you God-damn, impudent . . . Do you know who I am? Do you know that I can crush you like a cockroach, as I've crushed many a better—

STEVENS: [*With insulting calm*] That is just what I wanted to prove. That is all. Thank you, Mr. Whitfield.

FLINT: Your Honor! We move that the defense counsel's outrageous remark which led to this incident be stricken out!

JUDGE HEATH: The remark may go out.

[WHITFIELD *leaves the stand and sits down next to* NANCY LEE; *she takes his hand and holds it affectionately, showing great concern*]

FLINT: [*Loudly, solemnly*] The people rest.

STEVENS: Move that the case be dismissed for lack of evidence.

JUDGE HEATH: Denied.

STEVENS: Exception . . . Ladies and gentlemen of the jury! We cannot pass judgment on Karen

Andre without passing it on Bjorn Faulkner. He had put himself beyond all present standards; whether it was below or above them, is a question for each of us to decide personally. But I'll ask you to remember that he was the man who said he needed no justifications for his actions: *he* was the justification; the man who said that laws were made for the fun of breaking them. If you'll remember that, you will understand that the life into which he was thrown in his last few months was as impossible to him as that of a tiger in a vegetarian cafeteria. And to escape it, he would be driven to *the most desperate means*—including suicide!

[STEVENS *pauses, then calls*]

Our first witness will be James Chandler.

CLERK: James Chandler!

[CHANDLER, *middle-aged, precise, dignified, enters and takes the stand*]

You solemnly swear to tell the truth, the whole truth and nothing but the truth so help you God?

CHANDLER: I do.

STEVENS: Your name?

CHANDLER: James Chandler.

STEVENS: Your occupation?

CHANDLER: Handwriting expert of the New York Police Department.

[STEVENS *takes the letter read by* INSPECTOR SWEENEY *and hands it to* CHANDLER]

STEVENS: Do you recognize this letter?

CHANDLER: Yes. It is the letter found in Mr. Faulkner's penthouse on the night of his death. I have been called upon to examine it.

STEVENS: What were you asked to determine?

CHANDLER: I was asked to determine whether it was written by Mr. Faulkner.

STEVENS: What is your verdict?

CHANDLER: This letter was written by Bjorn Faulkner.

STEVENS: Your witness.

FLINT: Mr. Chandler, it has been called to your attention during the inquest that Miss Andre was in the habit of signing Faulkner's name to unimportant documents, at the time she was employed as his secretary. Have you compared those signatures with Faulkner's real ones?

CHANDLER: I have.

FLINT: What is your opinion of them?

CHANDLER: I can compliment Miss Andre on her art. The difference is very slight.

FLINT: With Miss Andre's knowledge of Mr. Faulkner, is it possible that she could have forged this letter so perfectly as to escape detection?

CHANDLER: It is not probable; but it is possible.

FLINT: That is all.

[CHANDLER *exits*]

STEVENS: Siegurd Jungquist!

CLERK: Siegurd Jungquist!

[JUNGQUIST *enters and takes the stand. He is a man in his late thirties, a little timid in a quiet, reserved way, with a naive face and questioning, as if constantly wondering, eyes. He is Swedish and speaks with an accent*]

CLERK: Do you solemnly swear to tell the truth, the whole truth and nothing but the truth so help you God?

JUNGQUIST: I do.

STEVENS: What is your name?

JUNGQUIST: Siegurd Jungquist.

STEVENS: What is your occupation?

JUNGQUIST: My last job was secretary to Herr Bjorn Faulkner.

STEVENS: How long have you held that job?

JUNGQUIST: Since beginning of November. Since Miss Andre left.

STEVENS: What was your position before that?

JUNGQUIST: Bookkeeper for Herr Faulkner.

STEVENS: How long did you hold that job?

JUNGQUIST: Eight years.

STEVENS: Did Mr. Faulkner give you Miss Andre's position when she was dismissed?

JUNGQUIST: Yes.

STEVENS: Did Miss Andre instruct you in your new duties?

JUNGQUIST: Yes, she did.

STEVENS: What was her behavior at that time? Did she seem to be angry, sorry or resentful?

JUNGQUIST: No. She was very calm, like always, and explained everything clearly.

STEVENS: Did you notice any trouble between Miss Andre and Mr. Faulkner at that time?

JUNGQUIST: [*Amused, with a kindly, but superior tolerance*] Herr Lawyer, there can be no more trouble between Herr Faulkner and Miss Andre as between you and your face in the mirror!

STEVENS: Have you ever witnessed any business conferences between Mr. Faulkner and Mr. Whitfield?

JUNGQUIST: I never been present at conferences, but I seen Herr Whitfield come to our office many times. Herr Whitfield he not like Herr Faulkner.

STEVENS: What makes you think that?

JUNGQUIST: I heard what he said one day. Herr Faulkner was desperate for money and Herr Whitfield asked him, sarcastic-like, what he was going to do if his business crash. Herr Faulkner shrugged and said lightly: "Oh, commit suicide." Herr Whitfield looked at him, very strangely and coldly, and said, very slowly: "If you do, be sure you make a good job of it."

[*An* ATTENDANT *enters and hands a note to* STEVENS. STEVENS *reads it, shrugs, astonished; then turns to* JUDGE HEATH]

STEVENS: If your Honor please, I would like to

report this incident which I consider as a hoax and whose purpose I would like to determine. A man has just called on the telephone and insisted on talking to me immediately. When informed that it was impossible, he gave the following message just brought to me.

[*Reads note*]

"Do not put Karen Andre on the stand until I get there." No signature.

[*The crash of her chair pushed back so violently that it falls makes all eyes turn to* KAREN. *She stands straight, eyes blazing, her calm poise shattered*]

KAREN: I want to go on the stand right away!

[*Reaction in the courtroom*]

FLINT: May I ask why, Miss Andre?

KAREN: [*Ignoring him*] Question me now, Stevens!

STEVENS: [*Very astonished*] I'm afraid it's impossible, Miss Andre. We have to finish the examination of Mr. Jungquist.

KAREN: Then hurry. Hurry.

[*She sits down, showing signs of nervousness for the first time*]

JUDGE HEATH: [*Rapping his gavel*] I shall ask the defendant to refrain from further interruptions.

STEVENS: Now, Mr. Jungquist, where were you on the night of January sixteenth?

JUNGQUIST: I was in our office in the Faulkner Building. I was working. I been working late for many nights.

STEVENS: What did you do when you heard of Mr. Faulkner's death?

JUNGQUIST: I want to call Herr Whitfield. I telephone his home in Long Island, but butler say he not home. I call his office in town, but no answer, no one there. I call many places, but not find Herr Whitfield. Then, I call his home again and I have to tell Mrs. Faulkner that Herr Faulkner committed suicide.

STEVENS: And when you told her that, what were Mrs. Faulkner's first words?

JUNGQUIST: She said: "For God's sake, don't give it to the newspapers!"

STEVENS: That is all.

[KAREN *jumps up, ready to go on the stand*]

FLINT: Just one moment please, Miss Andre. Why such hurry? Whom are you expecting?

[KAREN *sits down reluctantly, without answering*]

Mr. Jungquist, you have been employed by Bjorn Faulkner for over eight years, haven't you?

JUNGQUIST: Yes.

FLINT: Did you know all that time how crooked and criminal your boss's operations were?

JUNGQUIST: No, I did not.

FLINT: Do you know now that he was a criminal and a swindler?

JUNGQUIST: [*With the quiet dignity of a strong conviction*] No, I do not know *that*.

FLINT: You don't, eh? And you didn't know what all those brilliant financial operations of his were?

JUNGQUIST: I knew that Herr Faulkner did what other people not allowed to do. But I never wonder and I never doubt. I know it was not wrong.

FLINT: How did you know that?

JUNGQUIST: Because he was Herr Bjorn Faulkner.

FLINT: And he could do no wrong?

JUNGQUIST: Herr Lawyer, when little people like you and me meet a man like Bjorn Faulkner, we take our hats off and we bow, and sometimes we take orders; but we don't ask questions.

FLINT: Splendid, my dear Mr. Jungquist. Your devotion to your master is worthy of admiration. You would do anything for him, wouldn't you?

JUNGQUIST: Yes.

FLINT: Are you very devoted to Miss Andre, too?

JUNGQUIST: [*Significantly*] Miss Andre was dear to Herr Faulkner.

FLINT: Then such a little matter as a few lies for your master's sake would mean nothing to you?

STEVENS: We object, your Honor!

JUDGE HEATH: Objection sustained.

JUNGQUIST: [*With quiet indignation*] I not lied, Herr Lawyer. Herr Faulkner is dead and cannot tell me to lie. But if I had choice, I lie for Bjorn Faulkner rather than tell truth for you!

FLINT: For which statement I am more grateful than you can guess, Herr Jungquist. That is all.

[JUNGQUIST *exits*]

STEVENS: [*Solemnly*] Karen Andre!

[KAREN *rises. She is calm. She steps up to the stand with the poise of a queen mounting a scaffold. The* CLERK *stops her*]

CLERK: You solemnly swear to tell the truth, the whole truth and nothing but the truth so help you God?

KAREN: [*Calmly*] That's useless. I'm an atheist.

JUDGE HEATH: The witness has to affirm regardless.

KAREN: [*Indifferently*] I affirm.

STEVENS: What is your name?

KAREN: Karen Andre.

STEVENS: What was your last position?

KAREN: Secretary to Bjorn Faulkner.

STEVENS: How long have you held that position?

KAREN: Ten years.

STEVENS: Tell us about your first meeting with Bjorn Faulkner.

KAREN: I answered his advertisement for a stenographer. I saw him for the first time in his office, on an obscure side street of Stockholm. He was alone. It was my first job. It was his first office.

STEVENS: How did Faulkner greet you?

KAREN: He got up and didn't say a word. Just stood and looked at me. His mouth was insulting even when silent; you couldn't stand his gaze very long; I didn't know whether I wanted to kneel or slap his face. I didn't do either. I told him what I had come for.

STEVENS: Did he hire you then?

KAREN: He said I was too young and he didn't like me. But he threw a stenographer's pad at me and told me to get down to work, for he was in a hurry. So I did.

STEVENS: And you worked all day?

KAREN: All day. He dictated as fast—almost faster than he could talk. He didn't give me time to say a word. He didn't smile once and he never took his eyes off me.

STEVENS: When did he first

[*He hesitates*]

KAREN: When did he first take me? That first day I met him.

STEVENS: How did that happen?

KAREN: He seemed to take a delight in giving me orders. He acted as if he were cracking a whip over an animal he wanted to break. And I was afraid.

STEVENS: Because you didn't like that?

KAREN: Because I liked it . . . So when I finished my eight hours, I told him I was quitting. He looked at me and didn't answer. Then he asked me suddenly if I had ever slept with a man. I

said, No, I hadn't. He said he'd give me a thousand kroner if I would go into the inner office
and take my skirt off. I said I wouldn't. He said
if I didn't, he'd take me. I said, try it. He did.
. . . After a while, I picked up my clothes; but I
didn't go. I stayed. I kept the job.

STEVENS: And you worked, and lived, and rose to
success together ever since?

KAREN: For ten years. When we made our first
million kroner, he took me to Vienna. We sat in
a restaurant where the orchestra played "Sing,
Gypsy." When we made ten million, he took me
to Delhi. We stood on the shore of the Ganges,
on the steps of an old temple where men had
been sacrificed to gods . . . When we made
twenty-five million, he took me to New York.
We hired a pilot to fly a plane above the city—
and the wind waved Bjorn's hair as a banner over
the world at his feet.

STEVENS: Can you tell us the extent of Mr.
Faulkner's personal fortune at the height of his
success?

KAREN: No, and he couldn't tell you himself: he
had no personal fortune. He took what he
wanted. When he owed money to one of his
companies—it was crossed off the books and deb-
ited to the accounts of several other concerns.
It was very simple. We prepared all the balance
sheets ourselves.

STEVENS: Why did a man of Mr. Faulkner's genius
resort to such methods?

KAREN: He wanted to build a gigantic net and to
build it fast; a net over the world, held in his

own hand. He had to draw unlimited sums of money; he had to establish his credit. So he paid dividends out of his capital, dividends much higher than we actually earned.

STEVENS: When did Mr. Faulkner's business difficulties start?

KAREN: Over a year ago.

STEVENS: What brought Mr. Faulkner to America, this time?

KAREN: A short term loan of ten million dollars from the Whitfield National Bank was due and we could not meet it. We had to have an extension. Whitfield refused it. Until his daughter came into the question.

STEVENS: How did that happen?

KAREN: Bjorn met her at a party. She made it obvious that she was greatly interested in him . . . Then, one day, he came to me and said: "Karen, we have only one piece of collateral left and you're holding it. You'll have to let me borrow it for a while." I said: "Certainly. What is it?" He said it was himself. I asked: "Nancy Whitfield?" and he nodded. I didn't answer at once—it wasn't very easy to say—then, I said: "All right, Bjorn." He asked: "Will that change things between us?" I said: "No."

STEVENS: Had Mr. Faulkner proposed to Miss Whitfield?

KAREN: No. She had proposed to him.

STEVENS: How did that happen?

KAREN: He told me about it. She took him for a

drive and stopped on a lonely road. She said
that they were lost, that she had kidnapped
him and wouldn't release him. He answered
that the ransom she wanted was not in circulation. Then she turned to him pointblank and
said: "What's the use of pretending? I want
you and you know it. You don't want me and I
know that. But I pay for what I want, and I
have the price." He asked: "And what is the
price?" She said: "The extension of a certain
ten million dollar loan which you'll need to save
your business. If you stay out of jail as a swindler, it can be only in the custody of *Mrs. Bjorn
Faulkner!*"

[NANCY LEE *jumps up, trembling with indignation*]

NANCY LEE: It's a lie! It's a shameless lie! How can
you—

JUDGE HEATH: [*Striking his gavel*] Quiet, please!
Anyone disturbing the proceedings will be asked
to leave the courtroom!

[WHITFIELD *whispers to* NANCY LEE *and forces
her to sit down, patting her hand*]

STEVENS: What was Mr. Faulkner's answer to that,
Miss Andre?

KAREN: He said: "It will cost you an awful lot of
money." She answered: "Money has never
meant anything to me." Then he said: "Will you
always remember that it's a business deal?
You're not buying any feeling; you're not to
expect any." And she answered: "I don't need
any. You'll have your money and I'll have you."
Such was the bargain.

STEVENS: Was Mr. Whitfield eager to accept that bargain?

KAREN: Bjorn said he thought Mr. Whitfield would have a stroke when his daughter's decision was announced to him. But Miss Whitfield insisted. She always had her way. It was agreed that the loan would be extended and that Whitfield would give Bjorn unlimited credit.

STEVENS: In other words, Faulkner sold himself as his last security?

KAREN: Yes. And like the others, it meant nothing to him.

STEVENS: Did you resent that marriage?

KAREN: No. I didn't. We had always faced our business as a war. We both looked at this as our hardest campaign.

STEVENS: Why did Mr. Faulkner dismiss you two weeks after his wedding?

KAREN: He was forced to do that. Whitfield refused to advance the money he had promised.

STEVENS: What reason did he offer for that refusal?

KAREN: The reason that Bjorn was keeping a mistress. It was Miss Whitfield's ultimatum: I had to be dismissed.

STEVENS: And did Mr. Whitfield grant the loan after you were dismissed?

KAREN: No. He refused it again. He attached what he called "a slight condition" to it.

STEVENS: What was that condition?

KAREN: He wanted the controlling interest in Bjorn's enterprises.

STEVENS: Did Faulkner agree to that?

KAREN: Bjorn said that he'd rather gather all his stock certificates into one pile—and strike a match.

STEVENS: And did Mr. Whitfield grant the loan?

KAREN: No, he didn't grant it. Bjorn took it.

STEVENS: How did he do that?

KAREN: By forging Mr. Whitfield's signature on twenty-five million dollars' worth of securities.

STEVENS: How do you know that?

KAREN: [*Calmly*] I helped him to do it.

[*Reaction in the courtroom.* STEVENS *is taken aback;* FLINT *chuckles*]

STEVENS: Did this help Mr. Faulkner?

KAREN: Only temporarily. Certain dividend payments were coming due. We couldn't meet them. Bjorn had stretched his credit to the utmost—and there was no more to be had.

STEVENS: How did Mr. Faulkner take this situation?

KAREN: He knew it was the end.

STEVENS: What were his plans?

KAREN: You don't find men like Bjorn Faulkner cringing before a bankruptcy commission. And you don't find them locked in jail.

STEVENS: And the alternative?

KAREN: He was not afraid of the world. He had defied its every law. He was going to leave it when and how he pleased. He was——

[*The spectators' door at left flies open. A tall, slender, light-eyed young man in traveling clothes rushes in*]

REGAN: I told you to wait for me!

[KAREN *leaps to her feet with a startled cry.* FLINT, WHITFIELD, *and several* OTHERS *jump up.* FLINT *exclaims.*]

FLINT: "Guts" Regan!

KAREN: [*Desperately*] Larry! Keep quiet! Please! Oh, please, keep quiet! You promised to stay away!

[JUDGE HEATH *raps his gavel—to no avail*]

REGAN: Karen, you don't understand, you don't——

KAREN: [*Whirling toward* JUDGE HEATH] Your Honor! I demand that this man not be allowed to testify!

FLINT: Why not, Miss Andre?

STEVENS: [*Rushing to* KAREN] Wait! Don't say a word!

KAREN: [*Ignoring him, shouting desperately over the noise*] Your Honor . . . !

REGAN: Karen!
[*To* STEVENS]
Stop her! For God's sake, stop her!

JUDGE HEATH: Silence!

KAREN: Your Honor! This man loves me! He'll do *anything* to save me! *He'll lie!* Don't believe a word he says!
[*She breaks off abruptly, looks at* REGAN *defiantly*]

REGAN: [*Slowly*] Karen, your sacrifice is useless: Bjorn Faulkner is dead.

KAREN: [*It is a wild, incredulous cry*] He's . . . dead?

REGAN: Yes.

KAREN: Bjorn . . . dead?

FLINT: Didn't you know it, Miss Andre?
[KAREN *does not answer. She sways and falls, unconscious, on the steps of the witness stand. Pandemonium in the courtroom*]

CURTAIN

Act Three

Scene: *Same scene as at the opening of Acts I and II. Court session ready to open.* NANCY LEE, WHITFIELD, *and* JUNGQUIST *occupy the spectators' seats.* KAREN *sits at the defense table, her head bowed, her arms hanging limply. Her clothes are black. She is calm—a dead, indifferent calm. When she moves and speaks, her manner is still composed; but it is a broken person that faces us now. The* BAILIFF *raps.*

AILIFF: Court attention!

[JUDGE HEATH *enters.* EVERYONE *rises*]

Superior Court Number Eleven of the State of New York. The Honorable Judge William Heath presiding.

[JUDGE HEATH *sits down.* BAILIFF *raps and* EVERYONE *resumes his seat*]

JUDGE HEATH: The people of the State of New York versus Karen Andre.

STEVENS: Ready, your Honor.

93

FLINT: If your Honor please, I want to report that I have issued a warrant for Regan's arrest, as he is obviously an accomplice in this murder. But he has disappeared. He was last seen with the defense counsel and I would like to—

REGAN: [*Entering*] Keep your shirt on!
[*He walks toward* FLINT *calmly*]
Who's disappeared? What do you suppose I appeared for, just to give you guys a thrill? You don't have to issue any warrants. I'll stay here. If she's guilty, I'm guilty.
[*He sits down at the defense table*]

JUDGE HEATH: The defense may proceed.

STEVENS: Karen Andre.

[KAREN *walks to the witness stand. Her grace and poise are gone; she moves with effort*]

Miss Andre, when you took the stand yesterday, did you know the whole truth about this case?

KAREN: [*Faintly*] No.

STEVENS: Do you wish to retract any of your testimony?

KAREN: No.

STEVENS: When you first took the stand, did you intend to shield anyone?

KAREN: Yes.

STEVENS: Whom?

KAREN: Bjorn Faulkner.

STEVENS: Do you still find it necessary to shield him?

KAREN: [*Speaking with great effort*] No . . . it's not necessary . . . any more.

STEVENS: Do you still claim that Bjorn Faulkner committed suicide?

KAREN: No.
[*Forcefully*]
Bjorn Faulkner did not commit suicide. He was murdered. I did not kill him. Please, believe me. Not for my sake—I don't care what you do to me now—but because you cannot let *his* murder remain unpunished! I'll tell you the whole truth. I've lied at the inquest. I've lied to my own attorney. I was going to lie here—but everything I told you so far has been true. I'll tell you the rest.

STEVENS: You had started telling us about Mr. Faulkner's way out of his difficulties, Miss Andre.

KAREN: I told you that he was going to leave the world. But he was not to kill himself. I did throw a man's body off the penthouse. But that body was dead before I threw it. It was not Bjorn Faulkner.

STEVENS: Please explain this to us, Miss Andre.

KAREN: Bjorn wanted to be officially dead. No searches or investigations were to bother him. He was to disappear. That suicide was staged. He had had the plan in mind for a long time. He had kept ten million dollars of the Whitfield forgery for this. We needed someone to help us.

Someone who could not be connected with Bjorn in any way. There was only one such person: Regan.

STEVENS: What made you believe that Mr. Regan would be willing to help in so dangerous an undertaking?

KAREN: He loved me.

STEVENS: And he agreed to help you in spite of that?

KAREN: He agreed *because* of that.

STEVENS: What was the plan, Miss Andre?

KAREN: Regan was to get a corpse. But he wasn't to kill anyone for the purpose. We waited. On the night of January sixteenth, "Lefty" O'Toole, a gunman, was killed by rival gangsters. His murderers have since been arrested and have confessed, so you can be sure that Regan had nothing to do with the murder. But you may remember reading in the papers that O'Toole's body disappeared mysteriously from his mother's house. *That* was Regan's work. O'Toole's height, measurements and hair were the same as Bjorn's. He was the man I threw off the penthouse.

STEVENS: Was that the extent of Mr. Regan's help?

KAREN: No. He was to get an airplane and take Bjorn to South America. Bjorn had never learned to operate a plane. Regan used to be a transport pilot . . . That day, January sixteenth, Bjorn transferred the ten million dollars to three banks in Buenos Aires, in the name of Ragnar Hedin. A month later, I was to meet him at the Hotel

Continental in Buenos Aires. Until then—the three of us were not to communicate with each other. No matter what happened, we were not to reveal the secret.

STEVENS: Tell us what happened on January sixteenth, Miss Andre.

KAREN: Bjorn came to my house, that night. I'll never forget his smile when he stepped out of the elevator: he loved danger. We had dinner together. At nine thirty we went to Regan's. He had O'Toole's body dressed in traveling clothes. We drove back to my house. Bjorn wanted to be seen entering the building. So I didn't use my key. I rang the door bell. We were dressed formally, to make it look like a gay party. Bjorn and Regan supported the body as if he were a drunken friend. The night watchman opened the door. Then we went up in the elevator.

STEVENS: And then what happened?

KAREN: Bjorn exchanged clothes with the corpse. He wrote the letter. Then they carried the body out and left it leaning against the parapet. Then ... then, we said goodbye.
[KAREN'S *voice is not trembling; she is not playing for sympathy; only the slightest effort in her words betrays the pain of these memories*]
Bjorn was to go first. He went down in the elevator. I stood and watched the needle of the indicator moving down, fifty floors down. Then it stopped. He was gone.

STEVENS: And then?

KAREN: Regan followed him a few minutes later.

They were to meet ten miles out of the city where Regan had left his plane. I stayed alone for an hour. The penthouse was so silent. I didn't want to wait out in the garden—with the corpse . . . the dead man that was supposed to be Bjorn. I lay on the bed in my bedroom. I took Bjorn's robe and buried my face in it. I could almost feel the warmth of his body. There was a clock by the bed and it ticked in the darkness. I waited. When an hour passed, I knew that the plane had taken off. I got up. I tore my dress—to make it look like a struggle. Then, I went to the garden—to the parapet. I looked down; there were so many lights . . . the world seemed so small, so far away . . . Then, I threw the body over. I watched it fall. I thought all of Bjorn's troubles went with it . . . I didn't know that . . . his life went, too.

STEVENS: That is all, Miss Andre.

FLINT: I must confess, Miss Andre, that there is not much left for me to do: you've done all my work yourself . . . Now, tell us, didn't Mr. Faulkner have a clear conception of the difference between right and wrong?

KAREN: Bjorn never thought of things as right or wrong. To him, it was only: you can or you can't. He always could.

FLINT: And yourself? Didn't you object to helping him in all those crimes?

KAREN: To me, it was only: he wants or he doesn't.

FLINT: You said that Bjorn Faulkner loved you?

KAREN: Yes.

FLINT: Did he ever ask you to marry him?

KAREN: No. What for?

FLINT: Don't you know that there are laws made for situations such as these?

KAREN: Laws made *by* whom, Mr. Flint? And *for* whom?

FLINT: Miss Andre, did your attorney warn you that anything you say here may be held against you?

KAREN: I am here to tell the truth.

FLINT: You loved Bjorn Faulkner?

KAREN: Yes.

FLINT: Such as he was?

KAREN: *Because* he was such as he was.

FLINT: *Exactly*, Miss Andre. Now what would you do if a woman were to take away from you the man you worshipped so insanely? If she appealed to his soul, not to his animal desires as you seem to have done so successfully? If she changed the ruthless scoundrel you loved into her own ideal of an upright man? Would you still love him?

STEVENS: Your Honor! We object!

JUDGE HEATH: Objection sustained.

KAREN: But I want to answer. I want the District Attorney to know that he is insulting Bjorn Faulkner's memory.

FLINT: You do? But you thought nothing of insulting him while he lived, by an affair with a gangster?

REGAN: [*Jumping up*] You damn—

KAREN: [*Calmly*] Don't, Larry.

[REGAN *sits down reluctantly*]

You're mistaken, Mr. Flint. Regan loved me. I didn't love him.

FLINT: And he didn't demand the usual . . . price, for his help?

KAREN: He demanded nothing.

FLINT: You were the only one who knew all the details of Faulkner's criminal activities?

KAREN: Yes.

FLINT: You had enough information to send him to jail at any time?

KAREN: I'd never do that!

FLINT: But you *could*, if you'd wanted to?

KAREN: I suppose so.

FLINT: Well, Miss Andre, isn't that the explanation of Faulkner's visits to you after his marriage? He had reformed, he wanted to avoid a crash. But *you* held it over his head. You could ruin his plans and expose him before he had made good for his crimes. Wasn't it fear, not love, that held him in your hands?

KAREN: Bjorn never knew the meaning of the word fear.

FLINT: Miss Andre, who knew about that transfer of ten million dollars to Buenos Aires?

KAREN: Only Bjorn, myself and Regan.

FLINT: *And* Regan! Now, Faulkner could have had perfectly legitimate business reasons for that transfer?

KAREN: I don't know of any.

FLINT: You mean, you *won't tell* of any. Now, Miss Andre, Bjorn Faulkner kept you in extravagant luxury for ten years. You enjoyed platinum gowns and other little things like that. You hated to change your mode of living. You hated to see him turn his fortune over to his investors—to see him poor—didn't you?

KAREN: I was never to see him poor.

FLINT: No! Of course not! Because you and your gangster lover were going to murder him and get the ten million no one knew about!

STEVENS: Your Honor! We object!

JUDGE HEATH: Sustained.

FLINT: You've heard it testified that Faulkner had no reason to commit suicide. He had no more reason to escape from the first happiness he'd ever known. And you hated him for that happiness! Didn't you?

KAREN: You don't understand Bjorn Faulkner.

FLINT: Maybe I don't. But let's see if I understand *you* correctly. You were raped by a man the first day you saw him. You lived with him for ten years in a brazenly illicit relationship. You defrauded thousands of investors the world over. You cultivated a friendship with a notorious gangster. You helped in a twenty-five million dollar forgery. You told us all this proudly, flaunting your defiance of all decency. And you don't expect us to believe you capable of murder?

KAREN: [*Very calmly*] You're wrong. Mr. Flint. I *am* capable of murder—*for Bjorn Faulkner's sake.*

FLINT: That is all, Miss Andre.

[KAREN *walks back to her seat at the defense table, calmly, indifferently*]

STEVENS: Lawrence Regan!

CLERK: Lawrence Regan!

[REGAN *takes the stand*]

You solemnly swear to tell the truth, the whole truth and nothing but the truth so help you God?

REGAN: I do.

STEVENS: What is your name?

REGAN: Lawrence Regan.

STEVENS: [*A little hesitantly*] What is your occupation?

REGAN: [*Calmly, with a faint trace of irony*] Unemployed.

STEVENS: How long have you known Karen Andre?

REGAN: Five months.

STEVENS: Where did you meet her?

REGAN: In Faulkner's office. I went there to . . . to do some business with him. I gave up the business, because I met his secretary.

STEVENS: How did you happen to become friendly with Miss Andre?

REGAN: Well, that first meeting wasn't exactly friendly. She wouldn't let me in to see Faulkner. She said I had enough money to buy orchids by the pound—and I had no business with her boss. I said I'd think it over—and went. I thought it over. Only, I didn't think of the business. I thought of her. The next day I sent her a pound of orchids. Ever see how many that makes? That's how it started.

STEVENS: Did you know of Miss Andre's relations with Mr. Faulkner?

REGAN: I knew it before I ever saw her. What of it? I knew it was hopeless. But I couldn't help it.

STEVENS: You never expected Miss Andre to share your feeling?

REGAN: No.

STEVENS: You never made any attempt to force it upon her?

REGAN: Do you have to know all that?

STEVENS: I'm afraid we do.

REGAN: I kissed her—once. By force. It was the night of Faulkner's wedding. She was alone. She was so unhappy. And I was so crazy about her.

She told me it was no use. I never wanted her to know. But she knew. We never mentioned it since.

STEVENS: When did Miss Andre first tell you of Faulkner's planned escape?

REGAN: About two weeks before we pulled it.

STEVENS: Was "Lefty" O'Toole one of your men?

REGAN: No.

STEVENS: Were you connected with his murderers in any way?

REGAN: No.

STEVENS: [*With a little hesitation*] You actually had no definite knowledge of his planned murder?

REGAN: [*With the same faint irony*] No. I just had a way of guessing.

STEVENS: What happened on the night of January sixteenth?

REGAN: It all worked as Miss Andre has told you. But she knows only half the story. I know the rest.

STEVENS: Tell us what happened after you left the penthouse.

REGAN: I left ten minutes after Faulkner. He had taken my car. I had one of my men leave another car for me at the door. I stepped on it—full speed.

STEVENS: Where did you go?

REGAN: To Meadow Lane. Ten miles out, in Kings County. I had left my plane there earlier in the evening. Faulkner was to get there first and wait for me.

STEVENS: What time did you get there?

REGAN: About midnight. There was a bright moon. I turned off the road and I could see tire tracks in the mud—where Faulkner's car had passed. I drove out into the lane. Then, I thought I'd lost my mind: the plane was gone.

STEVENS: What did you do?

REGAN: I searched around that lane for two hours. Faulkner's car was there—where we had agreed to hide it. It was empty, lights turned off, the key in the switch. I saw tracks on the ground—where the plane had taken off. But Faulkner couldn't fly it himself.

STEVENS: Did you search for any clues to this mystery?

REGAN: I searched like a bloodhound.

STEVENS: Did you find anything?

REGAN: I did. One thing. A car.

STEVENS: What kind of a car?

REGAN: It was hidden deep in the bushes on the other side of the lane. It was a big black sedan.

STEVENS: What did you do?

REGAN: I wanted to know whose car it was, so I smashed a window, crawled to the back seat and settled down to wait.

STEVENS: How long did you have to wait?

REGAN: The rest of that night.

STEVENS: And then?

REGAN: Then, the owner came back. I saw him coming. His face looked strange. He had no hat. His clothes were wrinkled and grease-spotted.

STEVENS: What did you do?

REGAN: I pretended to be asleep in the back seat. I watched him. He approached; opened the door. Then, he saw me. He gave a start and a yell as if he'd been struck in the heart. His nerves must have been jittery.

STEVENS: Then, what did you do?

REGAN: I awakened with a start, stretched, rubbed my eyes, and said: "Oh, it's you? Fancy, such a meeting!" I don't think he liked it. He asked: "Who are you? What are you doing here?" I said: "My name's Guts Regan—you may have heard it. I was in a little trouble and had to hide for a while. And finding this car here was quite a convenience." He said: "That's too bad, but I'll have to ask you to get out. I'm in a hurry."

STEVENS: Did you get out?

REGAN: No. I stretched and asked: "What's the hurry?" He said: "None of your business." I smiled and explained: "It's not for me. You see, it happens that a certain columnist is a friend of mine. He'll appreciate the story about a gentleman of your prominence found wandering in the wilderness at milkman time. But I'm sure he would like to have the whole story."

STEVENS: What did the man say?

REGAN: He said nothing. He took out a check book and looked at me. I shrugged and looked at him. Then, he said: "Would ten thousand dollars be a suitable token of appreciation to keep your mouth shut?" I said: "It'll do. Lawrence Regan's the name." He wrote out the check. Here it is.

[REGAN *produces a check and hands it to* STEVENS. *Reaction in the courtroom*]

STEVENS: [*His voice is tensely ominous*] I offer this check in evidence.

[*He passes the check to the* CLERK. CLERK *glances at it and gives a start*]

FLINT: [*Jumping up*] What's all this nonsense? Who was the man?

STEVENS: [*Solemnly*] Who was the man, Mr. Regan?

REGAN: Let the clerk read that check to you.

STEVENS: [*To* CLERK] Kindly read the check.

CLERK: [*Reading*] January seventeenth . . . Pay to the order of Lawrence Regan the sum of ten thousand dollars." Signed: "John Graham Whitfield."

[*Uproar in the courtroom.* WHITFIELD *jumps to his feet*]

WHITFIELD: It's an outrage!

FLINT: I demand to see that check!

JUDGE HEATH: [*Striking his gavel*] Silence! If there are any more interruptions of this kind, I shall order the courtroom cleared!

STEVENS: We offer this check in evidence!

FLINT: Objection!

JUDGE HEATH: Objection overruled. Admitted in evidence.

STEVENS: What did you do after you received this check, Mr. Regan?

REGAN: I put it in my pocket and thanked him. Then—I drew my gun and stuck it in his ribs, and asked: "Now, you lousy bastard, what did you do with Faulkner?" He opened his mouth like a fish choking and couldn't make a sound.

WHITFIELD: Your Honor! Is this man to be allowed to make such statements in public in my presence?

JUDGE HEATH: The witness is allowed to testify. If it is proved to be perjury, he will suffer the consequences. Proceed, Mr. Stevens.

STEVENS: What did he answer, Mr. Regan?

REGAN: At first, he muttered: "I don't know what you're talking about." But I jammed the gun harder and I said: "Cut it out! I've no time to waste. I'm in on it and so are you. Where did you take him?" He said: "If you kill me, you'll never find out."

STEVENS: Did you get any information out of him?

REGAN: Not a word. I didn't want to kill him— yet. He said: "If you expose me—you'll expose the fake suicide and Faulkner will be found." I asked: "Is he alive?" He said: "Go and ask him." I talked and threatened. It was no use. I let him go. I thought I could always get him.

STEVENS: Then, did you try to find Faulkner?

REGAN: I didn't lose a second. I rushed home, changed my clothes, grabbed a sandwich and an airplane—and flew to Buenos Aires. I searched. I advertised in the papers. I got no answer. No one called at the banks for Ragnar Hedin's millions.

STEVENS: Did you try to communicate about this with Miss Andre?

REGAN: No. We had promised to stay away from each other for a month. And she had been arrested—for Faulkner's murder. I laughed when I read that. I couldn't say a word—not to betray him if he were still alive. I waited.

STEVENS: What were you waiting for?

REGAN: February sixteenth—at the Hotel Continental in Buenos Aires. I set my teeth and waited every minute of every hour of that day. He didn't come.

STEVENS: Then?

REGAN: Then I knew he was dead. I came back to New York. I started a search for my plane. We found it. Yesterday.

STEVENS: Where did you find it?

REGAN: In a deserted valley in New Jersey, a hundred miles from Meadow Lane. I recognized the plane by the engine number. It had been landed and fire set to it.

STEVENS: Was the plane . . . empty?

REGAN: No. I found the body of a man in it.

STEVENS: Could you identify him?

REGAN: No one could. It was nothing but a burned

skeleton. But the height was the same. It was Faulkner . . . I examined the body—or what was left of it. I found two bullet holes. One—in a rib, over the heart. The other—straight through the right hand. He didn't die without putting up a fight. He must have been disarmed first, shot through the hand; then, murdered, defenseless, straight through the heart.

STEVENS: [*After a pause*] That's all, Mr. Regan.

FLINT: Just what is your . . . *business*, Mr. Regan?

REGAN: You'd like me to answer, wouldn't you?

STEVENS: We object, your Honor. The witness has a right not to answer that question.

JUDGE HEATH: Sustained.

FLINT: Mr. Regan, what do you do when prospective clients refuse to pay you protection?

REGAN: I'm legally allowed not to understand what you're talking about.

FLINT: Very well. You don't have to understand. May I question you as to whether you read the newspapers?

REGAN: You may.

FLINT: Well?

REGAN: Question me.

FLINT: Will you kindly state whether you read newspapers?

REGAN: Occasionally.

FLINT: Then did you happen to read that when Mr. James Sutton Vance, Jr., refused to pay protection to . . . a certain gangster, his magnificent country house in Westchester was destroyed by an explosion, just after the guests left, barely missing a wholesale slaughter? What was that, Mr. Regan, a coincidence?

REGAN: A remarkable coincidence, Mr. Flint: *just after the guests left.*

FLINT: Did you read that when Mr. Van Dorn refused to—

STEVENS: We object, your Honor! Such questions are irrelevant!

JUDGE HEATH: Sustained.

FLINT: So you had no ill feeling toward Mr. Faulkner for the . . . failure of your business with him?

REGAN: No.

FLINT: Now, Mr. "Guts"—I beg your pardon—Mr. *Lawrence* Regan, what would you do if someone were to take this woman you love so much—and rape her?

REGAN: I'd cut his throat with a dull saw.

FLINT: You would? And you expect us to believe that you, "Guts" Regan, gangster, outlaw, scum of the underworld, would step aside with a grand gesture and throw the woman you wanted into another man's arms?

STEVENS: Your Honor! We—

[STEVENS *is near the witness stand. Calmly and forcefully* REGAN *pushes him aside. Then, turns to* FLINT *and says very calmly, very earnestly*]

REGAN: I loved her.

FLINT: You did? Why did you allow Faulkner to visit her after his marriage?

REGAN: I had nothing to say about that.

FLINT: No? You two didn't hold a blackmail plot over his head?

REGAN: Got any proof of that?

FLINT: Her association with you is the best proof!

STEVENS: Objection!

JUDGE HEATH: Sustained.

FLINT: How did you kill Faulkner in the penthouse that night?

STEVENS: Objection!

JUDGE HEATH: Sustained.

FLINT: Where is your other accomplice, the man who played the drunk?

REGAN: I can give you his exact address: Evergreen Cemetery, Whitfield Family Memorial; which is the swankiest place poor Lefty's ever been.

FLINT: Now, let me get this clear: you claim that the man buried in Evergreen Cemetery is "Lefty" O'Toole, and the man you found in the burned plane is Bjorn Faulkner?

REGAN: Yes.

FLINT: And what is to prove that it isn't the other way around? Supposing you did steal O'Toole's body? What's to prove that you didn't stage that fantastic thing yourself? That you didn't plant the airplane and the body in New

Jersey and then appear with that wild story, in a desperate attempt to save your mistress? You've heard her tell us that you'd do anything for her; that you'd lie for her.

STEVENS: We object, your Honor!

JUDGE HEATH: Objection sustained.

FLINT: Where's your real proof, Mr. Regan?

REGAN: [*He looks straight at* FLINT *for a second. When he speaks, his manner is a startling contrast to his former arrogance and irony; it is simple, sincere; it is almost solemn in its earnestness*] Mr. Flint, you're a district attorney and I . . . well, you know what I am. We both have a lot of dirty work to do. Such happens to be life—or most of it. But do you think we're both so low that if something passes us to which one kneels, we no longer have eyes to see it? I loved her; she loved Faulkner. That's our only proof.

FLINT: That's all, Mr. Regan.

[REGAN *returns to the defense table*]

STEVENS: John Graham Whitfield!

[WHITFIELD *walks to the stand hurriedly, resolutely*]

Mr. Whitfield, would you object if I asked for an order to exhume the body buried in Evergreen Cemetery?

WHITFIELD: I would have no objection—but that body has been cremated.

STEVENS: [*slight emphasis*] I see. Mr. Whitfield, where were you on the night of January sixteenth?

WHITFIELD: I believe I was in New York, on business, that night.

STEVENS: Do you have any witnesses who can prove it?

WHITFIELD: Mr. Stevens, you must realize that I am not in the habit of providing myself with alibis. I've never had reason to keep track of my activities and to secure any witnesses. I would not be able to find them now.

STEVENS: How many cars do you own, Mr. Whitfield?

WHITFIELD: Four.

STEVENS: What are they?

WHITFIELD: One of them is a black sedan, as you are evidently anxious to learn. I may remind you that it is *not* the only black sedan in New York City.

STEVENS: [*Casually*] You have just returned from California by plane?

WHITFIELD: Yes.

STEVENS: You flew it yourself?

WHITFIELD: Yes.

STEVENS: You're a licensed pilot, then?

WHITFIELD: I am.

STEVENS: Now, that story of Mr. Regan's is nothing but a lie in your opinion, isn't it?

WHITFIELD: It is.

STEVENS: [*Changing his manner, fiercely*] Then, who wrote that ten thousand dollar check?

WHITFIELD: [*Very calmly*] I did.

STEVENS: Will you kindly explain it?

WHITFIELD: It is very simple. We all know Mr. Regan's profession. He had threatened to kidnap my daughter. I preferred to pay him off, rather than to take any chances on her life.

STEVENS: The check is dated January seventeenth. On that same day, you announced your offer of a reward for Regan's arrest, didn't you?

WHITFIELD: Yes. You realize that besides my civic duty, I also had my daughter's safety in mind and I wanted prompt action.

STEVENS: Mr. Whitfield, your daughter and your fortune are your most cherished possessions, aren't they?

WHITFIELD: They are.

STEVENS: Then what would you do to the man who took your money and deserted your daughter for another woman?

FLINT: We object, your Honor!

JUDGE HEATH: Objection sustained.

STEVENS: You hated Faulkner. You wanted to break him. You suspected his intention of staging suicide, didn't you? The words Mr. Jungquist heard you say prove it.

WHITFIELD: I suspected nothing of the kind!

STEVENS: And on January sixteenth, didn't you spend the day watching Faulkner?

WHITFIELD: Certainly not!

STEVENS: Weren't you trailing Faulkner in your black sedan? Didn't you follow him as soon as he left his penthouse, that night?

WHITFIELD: Fantastic! How could I have recognized him—supposing it were Faulkner leaving? Van Fleet, the detective, didn't.

STEVENS: Van Fleet wasn't watching for a trick. He had no suspicion of the plot. You had.

WHITFIELD: [*With magnificent calm*] My dear Mr. Stevens, how could I have known about the plot for *that night?*

STEVENS: Didn't you have any particular information about Faulkner's activities at the time?

WHITFIELD: None.

STEVENS: You heard of nothing unusual, that day?

WHITFIELD: Not a thing.

STEVENS: For instance, you did not hear that he transferred ten million dollars to Buenos Aires?

WHITFIELD: I never heard of it.

[*There is a scream, a terrifying cry, as of one mortally wounded.* JUNGQUIST *stands clutching his head, moaning wildly*]

JUNGQUIST: I killed him! I killed Bjorn Faulkner, God help me! I helped *that man* to kill him!
[*He points at* WHITFIELD, *then leaps to the* CLERK'S *desk, seizes the Bible and, raising it frantically over his head in a shaking hand, cries as if taking a solemn, hysterical oath*]
The whole truth, so help me God! . . . I didn't know! But I see it now!
[*He points at* WHITFIELD]
He killed Faulkner! Because he lied! He knew about the ten million dollars! Because I told him!

[STEVENS *rushes to him*]

FLINT: Now, look here, my man, you can't—

STEVENS: [*Hurriedly*] That's all, Mr. Whitfield.

FLINT: No questions.

[WHITFIELD *leaves the stand*]

STEVENS: Kindly take the stand, Mr. Jungquist.
[JUNGQUIST *obeys*]
You told Mr. Whitfield about that transfer?

JUNGQUIST: [*Hysterically*] He asked me many
times about the ten million—where it was
spent. I did not know it was a secret. That
day—I told him—about Buenos Aires. That day
—at noon—January sixteenth!

WHITFIELD: What kind of a frame-up is this?

STEVENS: You told Whitfield? At *noon*?

JUNGQUIST: I did, God have pity on me! I didn't
know! I would give my life for Herr Faulkner!
And I helped to kill him!

STEVENS: That's all.

FLINT: Were you alone with Mr. Whitfield when
you told him?

JUNGQUIST: [*Astonished*] Yes.

FLINT: Then it's *your* word against Mr. *Whitfield's?*

JUNGQUIST: [*Stunned by the sudden thought, feebly*]
Yes . . .

FLINT: That's all.

[JUNGQUIST *leaves the stand*]

STEVENS: The defense rests.

JUDGE HEATH: Any other witnesses?

FLINT: No, your Honor.

JUDGE HEATH: The defense may proceed with the closing argument.

STEVENS: Your Honor! Ladies and gentlemen of the jury! You are here to decide the fate of a woman. But much more than one woman is here on trial. Before you pronounce your verdict on Karen Andre, think of your verdict on Bjorn Faulkner. Do you believe that he was the kind of man who would bow, renounce and repent? If you do—she's guilty. But if you believe that in this sad, halfhearted world of ours a man can still be born with life singing in his veins; a scoundrel, a swindler, a criminal, call him anything, but still a conqueror—if you value a strength that is its own motor, an audacity that is its own law, a spirit that is its own vindication—if you are able to admire a man who, no matter what mistakes he may have made in form, had never betrayed his essence: his self-esteem—if, deep in your hearts, you've felt a longing for greatness and for a sense of life beyond the lives around you, if you have known a hunger which gray timidity can't satisfy—you'll understand Bjorn Faulkner. If you do —you'll understand the woman who was his priestess . . . Who is on trial in this case? Karen Andre? No! It's you, ladies and gentlemen of the jury, who are here on trial. It is your own souls that will be brought to light when your decision is rendered!

JUDGE HEATH: The District Attorney may now conclude the case.

FLINT: Your Honor! Ladies and gentlemen of the jury! For once, I agree with the defense counsel. Two different types of humanity are opposed in this case—and your verdict will have to depend on which side you choose to believe. You are asked—by the defense—to take the side of a swindler, a harlot and a gangster against a man who is a model of social responsibility and a woman who is everything the ideal of womanhood has been for centuries. On one side, you see a life of service, duty and unselfishness; on the other— a steamroller of sensual indulgence and egoistic ambition. I agree with the defense counsel that the judgment on this case will be passed deep within your own souls. If you believe that man is placed on earth for a purpose higher than his own enjoyment—if you believe that love is more than sexual indulgence, that love is not confined to your bedroom, but extends to your family and your fellow-men—if you believe that selfless service to others is still the most sacred ideal a man can aspire to—you will believe that simple virtue is more powerful than arrogance and that a man like Bjorn Faulkner would be brought to bow before it. Let your verdict tell us that none shall raise his head too high in defiance of our common standards!

JUDGE HEATH: Ladies and gentlemen of the jury, the Bailiff will now escort you to the jury room. I shall ask you to consider your verdict carefully. You are to determine whether Karen Andre is guilty or not guilty of the murder of Bjorn Faulkner.

[*The.* BAILIFF *escorts the* JURY *out of the court-room. Then the stage is blacked out. Then, one by one, a spotlight picks out of the darkness the different* WITNESSES, *who repeat the most significant lines of their testimony— a quick succession of contradicting statements, presenting both sides of the case, reviewing the case for the audience, giving it swift flashes of what the jury is considering.*

The pin spot illuminates only the faces of the witnesses, one after the other, in the following order]

DR. KIRKLAND: I was called to examine the body of Bjorn Faulkner. I found a body mangled to an extreme degree.

HUTCHINS: Well, he was a bit tight. He wasn't very steady on his feet. Mr. Faulkner and the other gentleman had to help him. They almost dragged him into the elevator.

VAN FLEET: She is hoisting a man's body up on the parapet. A man in evening clothes. Faulkner. He's unconscious. No resistance. She pushes him with all her strength. He goes over the parapet. Down. Into space.

SWEENEY: [*Reading*] "I found only two enjoyable things on this earth whose every door was open to me: my whip over the world and Karen Andre."

MAGDA: He had a platinum gown made for her . . . She wore it on her naked body . . . And if it burned her shameless skin, she laughed like the pagan she is, and he kissed the burn, wild like tiger!

NANCY LEE: We had renounced material concerns, with all their consequences: pride, selfishness, ambition, the desire to rise above our fellow-men. We wanted to devote our life to spiritual values. We were planning to leave the city, to be part of some modest community, to be like everyone else.

WHITFIELD: I had full confidence that my business acumen would have prevented the crash—had Faulkner lived.

CHANDLER: It is not probable that the letter was forged; but it is possible.

JUNGQUIST: Herr Faulkner shrugged and said lightly: "Oh, commit suicide." Herr Whitfield looked at him and said, very slowly: "If you do, be sure you make a good job of it!"

KAREN: Bjorn Faulkner never thought of things as right or wrong. To him it was only: you can or you can't. He always could. To me it was only: he wants or he doesn't.

REGAN: But do you think we're both so low that if something passes us to which one kneels, we no longer have eyes to see it? I loved her; she loved Faulkner. That's our only proof.

[*After the last flash, the stage remains dark for a few seconds. Then the lights come on and the* JURY *returns into the courtroom*]

BAILIFF: Attention of the Court!

CLERK: The prisoner will rise and face the jury.
[KAREN *rises, head high*]
The jury will rise and face the prisoner. Mr. Foreman, have you reached a verdict?

FOREMAN: We have.

CLERK: What say you?

ENDING OF PLAY IF VERDICT IS "NOT GUILTY":

FOREMAN: Not guilty!
[KAREN *receives the verdict calmly. She raises her head a little higher and says slowly, solemnly*]

KAREN: Ladies and gentlemen, I thank you—in the name of Bjorn Faulkner.

CURTAIN

ENDING OF PLAY IF VERDICT IS "GUILTY":

FOREMAN: Guilty!

[KAREN *shows no reaction; she stands motionless.* STEVENS *jumps to his feet*]

STEVENS: We shall appeal the case!

KAREN: [*Calmly, firmly*] There will be no appeal. Ladies and gentlemen, I will not be here to serve the sentence. I have nothing to seek in your world.

CURTAIN